RICHARD ROHR is a globally recognized ecumenical teacher whose work is grounded in Christian mysticism, practices of contemplation and self-emptying, and compassion for the marginalized. He is a Franciscan priest of the New Mexico province and founder of the Center for Action and Contemplation (CAC) in Albuquerque, where he also serves as academic dean of the Living School for Action and Contemplation. Fr. Richard is the author of many books, including the bestsellers *Falling Upward, The Naked Now,* and *The Universal Christ*. The Center publishes Richard Rohr's Daily Meditations, free reflections emailed to hundreds of thousands of subscribers around the world.

PATRICK BOLAND is a consultant to the Center for Action and Contemplation who works directly with Richard Rohr on a number of projects, including the study guides to *The Universal Christ,* CAC's upcoming *Falling Upward* online course, and CAC's conference workshops. He lives near Dublin, Ireland, and is a psychotherapist and executive coach with an emphasis on team dynamics and integrated spirituality. Patrick's background is in education, theology, retreat leading, and leadership consulting.

cac.org

Twitter: @CACRadicalGrace

Every
Thing Is
Sacred

RICHARD ROHR
AND PATRICK BOLAND

Every Thing
Is Sacred

40 Practices and Reflections on
THE UNIVERSAL CHRIST

First published in the United States of America in 2021 by Convergent
Books, an imprint of Random House, a division of Penguin Random
House LLC, New York

First published in Great Britain in 2021

Society for Promoting Christian Knowledge
36 Causton Street
London SW1P 4ST
www.spck.org.uk

Portions of this work originally appeared in *The Universal Christ*, copyright
© 2019 Center for Action and Contemplation, Inc., published in Great
Britain by SPCK in 2019.

Unless otherwise stated, Richard Rohr uses his own translations and/or
paraphrases of Scripture. Father Richard draws from a variety of English
translations, including the Jerusalem Bible (JB), New American Standard
Bible (NASB), New English Translation (NET), J. B. Phillips New
Testament (Phillips), Revised Standard Version (RSV) and *The Message*. The
Center for Action and Contemplation's practice is to reference chapter and
verse for scriptural sources, but not to identify precise translations.

British Library Cataloguing-in-Publication Data
A catalogue record for this book is available from the British Library

ISBN 978-0-281-08616-0
eBook ISBN 978-0-281-08617-7

1 3 5 7 9 10 8 6 4 2

Typeset by Fakenham Prepress Solutions, Fakenham, Norfolk NR21 8NL
First printed in Great Britain by Jellyfish Print Solutions
Subsequently digitally printed in Great Britain

eBook by Fakenham Prepress Solutions, Fakenham, Norfolk NR21 8NL

Produced on paper from sustainable forests

For Fr. Frank and Danny, two kind, wise fathers who taught me to see God in all things.

And for Jess, whose very presence allows me to experience Love every day.

Contents

Introduction

Most of us are familiar with the saying "If you want something done, ask a busy person." There are many reasons certain people are in such great demand. I would add that if you want a job done *really well,* ask a person who both loves the message and trusts the messenger.

Patrick Boland has all three qualities: He is surely in demand, while being loving and trustful too, which you will clearly see in the pages ahead. Maybe the most direct way of saying it is that Patrick is a spiritual son to me—someone who really gets it!

It has to be divine providence that our staff here in New Mexico discovered Patrick all the way over in Ireland, and invited him here for a visit and a job interview some years ago. Once here, it seemed he could do about a dozen jobs really well! And although I hate to admit it, he got a good Jesuit theological education, which fully prepared him to deal critically with my Franciscan ideas.

At one point, he and I struck up a personal conversation. It went on for hours, as the layers of interest and affirmation bounced to and fro. *Who is this young man who gets the message so naturally?* I thought. *We need to talk further.* So we took a short road trip to Taos and then to San Felipe Indian Pueblo to attend their yearly feast day dances and to continue our common excitement under the wide blue sky.

I remember us both choking up as hundreds of earnest dancers came swarming into the plaza, wave upon wave, to the thunderous beat of drums and rattles. This was a living metaphor for the Universal Christ on full display right in front of us—the outpouring of God's presence in all of creation. The barefoot Natives seemed to recognize that the earth had to be touched directly and joyfully—and from all their extremities—to honor and show love inside God's first natural cathedral, the earth and the sky. Almost exactly like my barefoot Father, St. Francis, did.

This is incarnational Christianity! Not God reserved for a few but God available to all in a thousand, thousand visible forms, and celebrated, over and over. Not just a problem-solving forgiver-of-sins God but a God whose greatness made sin by comparison unattractive, undesirable, small, and stifling. Once God models *poured-out oneness* for us, we are on some level allured into doing the same. Growth by "attraction, not promotion," as the twelve-step program might say. Not so much a Christ coming *into* the world as coming *out of* a world that is already soaked with Presence.

And that is what both Patrick and I want you to experience for yourself in this little book. Not just warm thoughts but an entire earth and humanity warmed by the Word becoming flesh. This is a message you cannot know with your mind alone. You must come to know it in the very cells of your body—and see it in the cells of all bodies, which each carry the same divine DNA of their Creator. Think about it. How could they not be?

This book is neither pious nor academic but is filled with spiritual knowing waiting to be transferred to you if you have the right app (if you will allow me to use a mobile device metaphor). The app requires only two functions on your part—curiosity and a bit of love. Yet this book is not a workbook either because it is hardly work at all, nor does it ask for grinding concentration. We might just call it *A Guide to Christian Freedom and Fun! (But in a Quite Serious Way)*. Why not?

Honestly, what Patrick has brought together here is in many ways better than my original book, and I am not being humble or flattering. He is a natural peda-gogue and a bring-it-down-to-earth teacher. He knows how to pick out the key concepts, which are still often abstract in my theological mind, and make them sound and sing in your bones—which is surely what Jesus was talking about when he said that we needed to "love the Lord our God with our whole heart, soul, mind, and strength" (Mark 12:30). No heady, wordy, or textbook religion talks that way. Yet that is what Christianity usually became, except among many of the Celts. (Hmm, I wonder if you are making connections?)

Our hope is that this knowledge of the Universal Christ will not be stored away in disconnected theory but be connected to the here and now, and thus everywhere. One could conclude that we are not talking about religion at all but only about "life, and life more abundantly" (John 10:10). And God gives away Life through Life.

RICHARD ROHR
Albuquerque, New Mexico

How to Use This Book

My first encounter with Fr. Richard's work over a decade ago came as a most welcome surprise. I found a clarity, a humility, and a profound love in his teaching that encouraged me to embrace the deep beauty of God amid the uncertainties of life. Getting to know him over the last number of years has been an extraordinary gift, as his warmth, love, and presence—as well as razor sharp insight—have far surpassed any expectations I had.

When I spend time with Fr. Richard, we often talk about the ways we move from mere head knowledge to embodied knowledge, from having ideas to experiencing those same ideas deep within our lives. Our hope is that we would not only see God in certain "holy" places but also perceive the Universal Christ in all of life and experience every thing as sacred. It's from this place of embodied knowing and incarnational seeing that this book of reflections is inspired.

To most benefit from this book, it will be helpful to have access to a copy of Fr. Richard's book *The Universal Christ.* You may wish to read or reread the book in its entirety before beginning these reflections. Alternatively, you may wish to read these reflections alongside *The Universal Christ.* Some of these reflections will ask you to revisit longer passages from the original book. At other times, you may want to return to a standalone section or a full chapter so as to remind yourself of the fuller context of what's covered in the reflection. (Page references for quotations from the paperback version of *The Universal Christ* appear in parentheses at the end of the relevant excerpt.)

You may also find it helpful to keep a journal as you read through this book. Each of the forty reflections features one or more reflective exercises at the end. Quite a few of these will ask you to record your thoughts and reflect on key moments from your life. Having all your written reflections in one place will help you trace your experiences of reading through this book.

The first three reflections draw on the appendixes from *The Universal Christ,* which invite you to reflect on the evolution of your worldview and your spiritual journey. I wanted to include these at the start of this book so you'll be aware of the personal lenses you're bringing to the rest of the book. These opening reflections are slightly longer than those that follow, and they contain some events from the time line of my life as an example for you to reflect on the events and perspectives that have shaped your life.

Several of the reflections look at themes that might be challenging if you have unhealed pain or trauma. In these reflections, I've included some self-care guidelines for you to read before engaging in the reflective exercises. If you sense any apprehension or discomfort in engaging with a reflective exercise, I would encourage you to simply skip ahead to the next reflection.

As you read through this book, you'll notice that one reflection will focus on a deeply personal or psychological topic from *The Universal Christ* and the next might focus on a big idea that influences your entire perspective on life and the cosmos. Alternating between personal and universal themes like this can be a little challenging, particularly if you are used to more sequential learning. My hope is that this approach serves as an invitation toward a contemplative way of reflecting, where you are "drawn forward into a much Larger Field" (page 6) without your egoic mind being totally in control. As Fr. Richard writes, it's an opportunity to explore "the cosmos you live inside of" (page 7) by paying attention to the interplay of your experiences, thoughts, feelings, and perceptions. Here you will have a chance to "recognize the Presence" (page 58) in each link of the "Great Chain of Being."

PATRICK BOLAND
Wicklow, Ireland

Every Thing Is Sacred

The Four Worldviews

Your worldview is not what you look at. It is what you *look out from or look through*. (page 241)

During our formative years, each of us has unique experiences that shape not only what we see in the world around us but also how we see reality. Our parents, our friends, our religious community, and our society all help to provide boundaries so that we can grow, develop, and make sense of our world. But, over time, as we mature and experience life in new ways, our original worldview is challenged. This can be painful, and if we've overidentified with our religious community and local cultural experiences, we can feel trapped: *If I continue to see the world through these lenses, I'll stagnate; but if I move on, I'll feel like I'm leaving my close friends, my church community, or even my family for good.* This binary "in-or-out" approach is common the first time our worldview is challenged.

As we begin to reflect on Fr. Richard's book *The Universal Christ,* it's important to take some time to explore the lenses that we use to perceive reality. Neuroscientific research shows us that we simply do not have the processing capacity, through our five senses and our brain, to take in all the data that is available to us each moment of our day.[1] So we reduce our moment-by-moment experiences to a manageable level. For example, we avoid thinking about how some of our economic pursuits are damaging our environment, or we generalize that certain politicians are always wrong, to the point where we can't hear them when they say something right.[2] When groups agree upon these pictures of reality, very powerful worldviews ensue.

In *The Universal Christ,* Fr. Richard outlines the four worldviews through which we engage with life, faith, and spirituality at different points in our journeys. "There are good things about all four of them," he wrote, "and none of them is completely wrong or completely right, but one of them is by far the most helpful" (page 242):

1. "Those who hold the *material worldview* believe that the outer, visible universe is the ultimate and 'real'

world. People of this worldview have given us science, engineering, medicine, and much of what we now call 'civilization.'. . . A material worldview tends to create highly consumer-oriented and competitive cultures, which are often preoccupied with scarcity, since material goods are always limited" (page 242).

2. "The *spiritual worldview* characterizes many forms of religion and some idealistic philosophies that recognize the primacy and finality of spirit, consciousness, the invisible world behind all manifestations. . . . But taken too far, it can become ethereal and disembodied, disregarding ordinary human needs and denying the need for good psychology, anthropology, or societal issues of peace and justice. The spiritual worldview, taken too seriously, has little concern for the earth, the neighbor, or justice, because it considers this world largely as an illusion" (page 242).

3. "Those holding . . . the *priestly worldview* are generally sophisticated, trained, and experienced people that feel their job is to help us put matter and Spirit together. They are the holders of the law, the scriptures, and the rituals; they include gurus, ministers, therapists, and sacred communities. People of the priestly worldview help us make good connections that are not always obvious between the material and spiritual worlds. . . . This view assumes that the two worlds are actually separate and need someone to bind them back together. . . .

It describes what most of us think of as organized religion and much of the self-help world" (pages 242–43).
4. "The *incarnational worldview* [is one] in which matter and Spirit are understood to have never been separate. Matter and Spirit reveal and manifest each other. *This view relies more on awakening than joining, more on seeing than obeying, more on growth in consciousness and love than on clergy, experts, morality, scriptures, or rituals. The code word I am using in this entire book for this worldview is simply 'Christ.'* . . . In Christian history, we see the *incarnational worldview* most strongly in the early Eastern Fathers, Celtic spirituality, many mystics who combined prayer with intense social involvement, Franciscanism in general, many nature mystics, and contemporary eco-spirituality" (page 243).

Over time, as we embrace the external changes that life brings, we need to make room for and pay attention to internal changes we experience. We let go of some aspects of one worldview and include other aspects from a different worldview. We slowly learn to hold the tension of embracing different worldviews at the same time.

REFLECTIVE EXERCISES

Spend some time reflecting on your own experiences of the four worldviews and the lenses through which you see reality today.

1. In a journal or on the page that follows, write out or circle the words that describe the aspects of each world–view with which you have resonated in the past.

1. MATERIAL	2. SPIRITUAL
• The outer, visible universe is the ultimate "real" world • **Gives us:** science, engineering, medicine • Consumer-oriented, competitive	• The "real" world is found in our inner, spiritual selves and the invisible world • **Gives us:** some psychology, esoteric New Age, reality of spirit world • Can be disembodied, denies the need to act on social justice issues or care for the earth
3. PRIESTLY	4. INCARNATIONAL
• The "real" world is found in structured practices and sophisticated rituals that bring matter and spirit together • **Gives us:** gurus, ministers, sacred communities, self-help, organized religion • Assumes a separation between matter and spirit	• The "real" world connects our inner lives with all that is visible and invisible, with others, and with the whole cosmos • **Gives us:** awakening, ways of seeing, growth in consciousness and love more than clergy, experts, morality, scriptures, or ritual • Amalgamates all three other worldviews, engages in everything from eco-spirituality to social involvement, "Christ"

2. Time Line of Worldviews in Your Life

Plot which of the four worldviews most resonated with you at various points in your life. The time line begins with your first memory and ends at your current age. You may find it helpful to write down a few words that summarize what was going on in your life at each of these stages.

PATRICK'S TIME LINE

```
0        5          12        16        26        30    Today
———|————|————|————|————|————>
```

• **Birth–age 5:** Incarnational—Safe, loving upbringing

• **Ages 5–12:** Priestly—First church experiences

• **Ages 12–16:** Material—Teenager, driven

• **Ages 16–26:** Spiritual—Depression, seeking meaning, reading Bible

• **Ages 26–30:** Spiritual + Incarnational—Relational loss and career disappointment, reordering of spiritual and life priorities

• **Age 30–today:** Incarnational—Embracing paradox, more comfortable with not knowing

YOUR TIME LINE

```
0                                                      Today
————————————————————————————————>
```

3. Notice the transition points on your time line. What experiences precipitated your moving from one worldview toward another? Journal as much detail as you can remember.

4. Reread the passage on the *incarnational worldview*, with Fr. Richard's note that "the code word I am using in this entire book for this worldview is simply 'Christ.'" Then journal your reflections on what it would be like to predominantly experience life from within this worldview.

The Pattern of Spiritual Transformation: Part I

We grow by passing beyond some perfect order, through a usually painful and seemingly unnecessary disorder, to an enlightened reorder or "resurrection." This is the "pattern that connects" and solidifies our relationship with everything around us. (page 247)

On first hearing, words like *growth* and *transformation* can sound optimistic and full of potential. Our contemporary lifestyle flouts the benefits of movement, agility, and the ability to "change and grow" in response to our environment. Nowhere was this more evident than during the initial weeks and months of the global coronavirus pandemic. Countries, communities, and businesses that quickly changed their behavior were able to adapt to this tragic new reality with the least loss of life. But even their "transformation" came with much suffering and at great cost, not only to the sick and the grieving but to the millions who lost their jobs and to the parents who had to juggle work while taking care of their kids at home.

As we seek to grow in our spiritual lives, we can easily forget that suffering is a prerequisite to experiencing true transformation. We need to be prepared to "take up our cross" and let go of old ways of seeing so that we can experience a new reality. Fr. Richard calls this moving "from *Order* to *Disorder* and then ultimately to *Reorder*" (page 248).

FROM ORDER TO DISORDER

When we experience shock, pain, and loss, it often leaves us struggling to make sense of our faith. We're deeply in love, but something unexpected happens with our partner; we believe we have a calling from God, but nobody supports what we're trying to do. We pray harder, attend church, and expectantly hope for things to return to what they once were or go the way we want them to. But if nothing changes, if our prayers go unanswered, we eventually move beyond our comfortable, stable worldview of spiritual order.

My own experience of disorder led me to embrace the *priestly worldview.* I studied theology and trained as both a psychotherapist and a coach. I remember sitting in silence during my first lectures on counseling, as we learned about the significance of family systems, the values we unconsciously learn from society, and how we respond after traumatic events. It was so different from the understanding of reality that I had often heard in church, where my job was to listen to God's Word, pray about every decision, and quickly forgive others and not dwell on past hurts.

Many of my friends, faced with similar disorder, embraced the *material worldview* instead. They abandoned their faith, relied almost solely on empirical facts, and focused on the rewards of a successful career in order to find a sense of meaning. While some stayed there, often remaining wounded by their former *spiritual worldview,* others experienced even more disorder within this *material worldview,* gave up, and "decided that 'there is no universal order'" (page 249).

Fr. Richard writes, "Even inside an incarnational worldview, we grow . . . through a usually painful and seemingly unnecessary disorder" (page 247). Although the *incarnational worldview* teaches us *about* this pattern of spiritual transformation, our lived experiences of loss and disorder are still difficult for our psyche to embrace. It often takes many cycles of loss before we begin to accept this "down-and-then-up"[1] pattern of spiritual transformation.

REFLECTIVE EXERCISES

Spend some time reflecting on how you have experienced order and disorder in your life.

1. Order: "At this first stage, *if we are granted it (and not all are),* we feel innocent and safe" (page 248).

Flip through an old family photo album or find some photos of when you were young. Take some time to connect with the memories of those experiences.

• What did you learn about the order of the world from your family, your schooling, your social life, and your religious experiences?
• Which aspects of the four worldviews (from Reflection 1) featured in your experiences of order?
• Journal your responses.

TIPS FOR JOURNAL WRITING

• You must write for yourself, knowing that nobody else will ever read this. You can even destroy the journal entry once you've finished writing, but take the time to really listen to yourself and to reflect.
• You may find it helpful to write to yourself in the second person (for example, "You were hoping this relationship would last, but . . .").

2. Disorder: "Eventually your ideally ordered universe—your 'private salvation project,' as Thomas Merton called it[2]—must and will disappoint you, *if you are honest*. As Leonard Cohen puts it, 'There is a crack in everything, that's how the light gets in'"[3] (pages 248–49).

• What life experiences, from any stage in your life, did you find disappointing or upsetting? Trust your intuition and go with the first thought that comes to mind.
• In your journal, write about what happened, how it left you feeling, and what impact the experience has on you today.

The Pattern of Spiritual Transformation: Part II

There is no nonstop flight to reorder. To arrive there, we must endure, learn from, and include the disorder stage, transcending the first naïve order— *but also still including it!* (page 250)

T he path from order through disorder to reorder, writes Fr. Richard, "is an insistence on going *through—not under, over, or around*" the disappointments we experience in life (page 250). We seek close friendships, intimate love, meaningful and well-paid work. When our grand plans don't work out, we're tempted to avoid the consequences of what ensues. We look for the easy way out, but there is no life hack and no fast track that quickly get us to the wisdom of reorder. No matter how often I repeat this cycle, the pain of disorder continues to sting and the emergence into reorder surprises me each time.

More than two millennia ago, Stoic philosophers talked about the importance of embracing disorder. This belief still influences us today, with everyone from psychotherapists[1] to business leaders and NFL linemen[2] preaching about the benefits of facing challenges head on. One of modern Stoicism's core messages is succinctly explained in the title of a recent book, *The Obstacle Is the Way: The Timeless Art of Turning Trials into Triumph*.[3]

But not all our experiences of reorder feel like triumph in the traditional sense of winning at something or beating others in a contest. In fact, Fr. Richard writes that reorder "is *given* more than it is created or engineered by us. . . . You are taken to happiness—you cannot find your way there by willpower or cleverness. Yet we all try!" (page 252). Reorder happens when we stop pushing and let go of the need to control the outcome. As a friend of mine often says, the path out of disorder requires you "to sit with the pain until it heals you." Only then are we ready to remove our old lenses and see the world anew.

Embracing reorder requires us to firstly let go of our illusions of order and control. It might even mean admitting that life is now different than what it once was or what we hoped it would be. We used to have a strong faith, but now we're just going through the motions of

church. We made career choices based on scarcity and a
desire for monetary safety rather than something more
fulfilling. What we hoped for from a marriage has simply
not come to pass. Fr. Richard writes that "we all come to
wisdom at the major price of both our innocence and
our control" (page 251). This is a really difficult path, one
that is painful for our ego to accept.

As a fifteen-year-old in religion class, I had wanted
clear black-and-white answers and despaired of the
teachers who used the word *mystery* as a response to my
difficult questions. Then personal disappointments, career confusion, and relational loss taught me the hard
lessons of disorder. I fought against the unfairness of it
all. As Fr. Richard writes, people "must somehow be
'wounded' before they give up these foundational illusions [of control]" (page 251). But there's good news,
even in this:

> Maintaining our initial order is not of itself hap-
> piness. We must expect and wait for a "second
> naïveté," which is *given* more than it is created
> or engineered by us. Happiness is the spiritual
> outcome and result of full growth and maturity,
> and this is why I am calling it "reorder." (pages
> 251–52)

Eventually, as my world was reordered, I slowly
learned to accept gray both-and answers and include

perspectives that I had previously excluded. I was surprised to notice that some long-lost boyhood spiritual practices began to resonate once more: simple things like lighting a prayer candle in a darkened church or making the sign of the cross. Practices I had left behind during the innocence of youth now took on a deep and inexplicable significance in this "second naïveté."

I learned that mystery doesn't mean that something is unknowable; it merely points to the fact that there are endless ways of seeing that same thing. My job is to let go of enough order and control so I can experience life's mysteries in full.

REFLECTIVE EXERCISES

1. From Disorder to Reorder

When have you experienced challenge, suffering, or disappointment from which you thought you'd never recover but through which you eventually made it and started to live life again?

• What was it like to eventually move on and see life from this new perspective?
• In what ways did this reorder of your world surprise you?

2. Time Line of the Patterns of Spiritual Transformation

Plot which of the three patterns of spiritual transformation (order, disorder, or reorder) were operating

at various points in your life. The time line begins with
your first memory and ends at your current age.

PATRICK'S TIME LINE

| 0 | 12 | 16 | 25 | 28 | Today |

—————|—————|—————|—————|——————>

- **Birth–age 12:** Order
- **Ages 12–16:** Disorder
- **Ages 16–18:** Reorder
- **Ages 18–25:** Order
- **Ages 25–28:** Disorder
- **Age 28–Present:** Reorder

YOUR TIME LINE

0   Today

————————————————————————————>

3. Turn back now to the time line you drew for Reflection 1—The Four Worldviews and consider the way
your worldview has been affected by the life experiences within both time lines.

   When you are ready, spend some time in silent
prayer/reflection on anything that comes up for you.

Christ Is Everywhere

> The Christ Mystery [is] the indwelling of the Divine Presence in everyone and everything since the beginning of time as we know it. . . . Christ is everywhere; in Him every kind of life has a meaning and has an influence on every other kind of life. (pages 1–3)

For Catholic boys and girls, the weeks leading up to their First Holy Communion can be a strange and anxious time. "Will I remember my prayers? Make sure to confess *all* your sins beforehand—you can't leave anything out. Don't *chew* the bread; it's the Body of Christ." I remember wondering whose body we'd actually be eating, Jesus or the Christ? Jesus seemed like the most wonderful man. I prayed to him a lot and was both sad and glad that he died for me. But I had my reservations about eating his body. My main concern was which part of his body I'd be eating. I hoped it wouldn't be his privates. Surely it would be a lot better to eat the "Body of Christ," like the priest said. To my six-year-old self, Christ seemed like a distant enough figure that eating him would be just fine.

It was here that my confusion between the person of Jesus and the cosmic nature of the Christ began. Jesus Christ was a human being who lived on earth, but he was also part of the Trinity, along with the Father and the Holy Spirit, wasn't he? It was so confusing to my young mind. Like many others, I decided to focus on the human aspect of this part of the Trinity. After all, Jesus had a first name, he liked children, and he told good stories. That all made sense. From then on, apart from hearing the word *Christ* mentioned at Mass, I never thought about Jesus's "other name."

Fr. Richard writes that many of us have done something similar. "We gradually limited the Divine Presence to the single body of Jesus, *when perhaps it is as ubiquitous as light itself—and uncircumscribable by human boundaries*" (page 4).

Such a deep and broad vision of Divine Presence is beyond the way we normally think. We *need* to categorize our experiences in order to make sense of daily life, and we describe these categories in phrases like "she's a glass-half-empty kind of person," "every cloud has a silver lining," or "I'm just not the creative type." Lenses like these can limit our growth, or they can help us see the deeper, broader, ubiquitous nature of the Universal Christ.

We need to pay attention to these lenses that we use. Fr. Richard writes, "Truly enlightened people see oneness because they *look out from oneness,* instead of labeling everything as superior and inferior, in or out" (page 7). But looking out from oneness requires us to first look in. We must start by examining how we separate and divide our interior world, including our own self-image, into different parts. If we don't begin here, we will have a tough time seeing "a cosmic notion of the Christ [that] competes with and excludes no one, but includes everyone and everything (Acts 10:15, 34)" (page 7).

If we allow this vision of Christ to permeate our vision of ourselves, we come to see that "all is anointed" (page 20): the flowers and trees, the cities and stores, all animals and all people. Surely this is an enchanted way of seeing the world, to see everything as "a miracle" (page 7).

Little boys and girls—and adults of all backgrounds—need no longer worry about eating the Body of Christ. If we are open to shifting our focus, we might see that Christ is everywhere and in *every thing.*

REFLECTIVE EXERCISE

Read the following excerpts from a prayer attributed to St. Patrick in 433 CE. Sit with the prayer awhile, reading it several times in a contemplative way. Instead of analyz–ing each line, pay attention to the words, phrases, and images that most speak to you, even if you don't fully understand why. As Fr. Richard writes, *"Contemplation is waiting patiently for the gaps to be filled in, and it does not insist on quick closure or easy answers"* (page 8).

St. Patrick's Breastplate

TRANSLATED BY KUNO MEYER

I arise to-day
Through the strength of heaven;
Light of sun,
Radiance of moon,
Splendour of fire,
Speed of lightning,
Swiftness of wind,
Depth of sea,
Stability of earth,
Firmness of rock . . .

Christ with me, Christ before me, Christ behind me,
Christ in me, Christ beneath me, Christ above me,
Christ on my right, Christ on my left,

Christ when I lie down, Christ when I sit down, Christ
  when I arise,
Christ in the heart of every man who thinks of me,
Christ in the mouth of every one who speaks of me,
Christ in every eye that sees me,
Christ in every ear that hears me.

Allow the prayer to settle within you and then, when you're ready, journal about the thoughts, emotions, or physical sensations it evokes.

Contemplation

Especially as we begin, we must allow some of the words in this book *to remain partially mysterious, at least for a while.* I know this can be dissatisfying and unsettling to our egoic mind, which wants to be in control every step of the way. Yet this is precisely the contemplative way of reading and listening, and thus being drawn forward into a much Larger Field. (page 6)

The contemplative way of listening that Fr. Richard describes in this passage has been the experience of billions of people during the global coronavirus pandemic. Such a painful and distressing time epitomizes the collective loss of control and the challenge that most of us have in embracing uncertainty. We are forced to "wait" in a way that is alien to many of us: wait to see loved ones, to receive test results, to return to school, and to find out when we can go back to life "as normal" again. If you have lived through the challenges of the 2007–08 financial crisis or have come through the tense hours of a major storm or fire, you have experienced something similar.

Fr. Richard tells us that in order to gain a new understanding of the world in times of great uncertainty, we have to "proceed by indirection, by waiting, and by the practice of attentiveness" (page 6). We have to wait "*patiently for the gaps to be filled in*" (page 8). This contemplative way of living, holding the tension of the unknown, is exactly what Fr. Richard invites us into as we "allow some of the words in this book *to remain partially mysterious, at least for a while*" (page 6).

Contemplation is a way of seeing and a way of experiencing life. We engage in contemplative practices, such as a contemplative sit, so we can practice moving beyond our ego's drive for certainty and control. Engaging in a contemplative sit requires us to first acknowledge our tendency to categorize each momentary experience. We then choose to enter a prayerful time of silence that quiets our minds and helps us open ourselves to what we do not already know. As we engage our whole bodies, becoming aware of our emotions and thoughts, we seek to move beyond their momentary bids for our attention so that we can be more aware of God's presence.

As Fr. Richard says, "Contemplation is an exercise in failure." This is because each time we pray, and despite "our best intentions to remain present to Presence, our habitual patterns of thinking and feeling interrupt and distract. Yet it is the desire that matters. Through our repeated failings we encounter God's grace."[1]

Contemplative practices have existed within the Christian tradition for almost two millennia, beginning with Origen of Alexandria (circa 186–251 CE) and his teachings on how to pay attention during prayer. These practices developed through the Desert Mothers and Fathers on into Celtic spirituality, and were aided by teachers such as Meister Eckhart and Julian of Norwich and by classic books on the subject such as *The Cloud of Unknowing,* to name but a few. After a centuries-long reprieve precipitated by the Reformation, well-known teachers such as Thomas Merton and Thomas Keating helped return contemplative practices to the West in the twentieth century. These teachers sought to help people toward an embodied experience of unity *with* God rather than a merely cognitive knowledge *about* God.

No matter how much we know about Scripture, liturgy, or theology, the uncertainties of tomorrow and the complexities of our relationships, hurts, and hopes all invite us beyond a merely cognitive faith. We need to learn ways of holding the tension within these complex situations that we cannot totally control. Contemplation helps us look out on the world with a humble attitude of accepting that we will never fully know and that there will always be more to see, more to learn, more ways to experience God. But instead of growing despondent at this awareness, contemplation helps us focus our attention on our lived experiences in *this* moment.

When I embrace this way of reading Scripture or paying attention to God's presence, my egoic mind (the part of me that wants "to be in control every step of the way") loses some of its power. I no longer need definitive answers that align with my preferences, habits, and the worldview I've constructed that makes me feel safe and secure. I'm proceeding "by indirection, by waiting, and by the practice of attentiveness" (page 6).

REFLECTIVE EXERCISE

Read through any one of the italicized passages in the first chapter of *The Universal Christ* ("Before We Begin"). Attempt to read it in a contemplative way:

• Settle down in a quiet place, taking a break from technology and other distractions.
• Take a few breaths and prayerfully express your desire to be open to whatever ways God might speak to you through this passage.

• Slowly read the passage two or three times, with pauses in between each reading.

• By the second or third reading, notice whether there is a particular word or phrase that stands out to you.

• Journal what comes to mind: the memories you recall, the emotions you feel, the thoughts you have. How is this passage related to your life right now? You may want to journal some more or pray.

• Read the passage one final time and take a few moments of silence before returning to the rest of your day.

The First Incarnation

This self-disclosure of whomever you call God into physical creation was the *first Incarnation.* . . . To put this idea in Franciscan language, *creation is the First Bible, and it existed for 13.7 billion years before the second Bible was written.* (page 12)

There's a stony cove that looks out over a small bay near where I live. Whenever I can, I take out my paddleboard on a summer's evening and paddle a few hundred meters offshore until I can see the mountains lifting their heads above the sheer cliffs that line the mile-long beach. One gray seal regularly pops her head up to say hi as I steady my balance over the waves. Arriving at the cliffs beyond the beach, I'm alone with the guillemots, a colony of cormorants, and the occasional leap of mackerel. The birds make their warning calls, and we all agree to go quiet and sit and wait. We watch one another from a short distance, with only the gentle lapping of waves occasionally breaking our silence. Such natural, wild beauty reminds me that

> *Everything visible, without exception, is the outpouring of God.* What else could it really be? "Christ" is a word for the Primordial Template (*"Logos"*) through whom "all things came into being, and not one *thing* had its being except through him" (John 1:3). (page 13)

I glance west and see the Great Sugar Loaf, a small volcano-shaped mountain that faces a large stately home called Powerscourt House. It was here, in the 1830s, that John Nelson Darby first taught that a rapture would take place, where Christians would be bodily taken up to the clouds to meet the Lord at the Second Coming of Christ. His dispensationalist theology emphasized the fallen nature of our planet and suggested that we should shift our focus to a new heaven and new earth. Darby's theology was most warmly received in North America, where it was adopted among a wide array of Christian denominations. As this view of the world evolved, it shifted the emphasis from the beauty of the first Incarnation to something entirely different. "Ironi-

cally, millions of the very devout who are waiting for
the 'Second Coming' have largely missed the first . . ."
"Sadly, we have a whole section of Christianity that is
looking for—even praying for—an exit from God's ongoing creation toward some kind of Armageddon or
Rapture. Talk about missing the point!" (page 20).

How influenced are we, I wonder, by this idea of
escape? How conscious are we of this narrative that tells
us our beautiful biosphere, this *first Incarnation,* is essentially fallen—beyond repair and in need of version 2.0?
Perhaps this has affected our attitude toward the earth's
resources, where our behavior displays where our true
values lie. Fr. Richard writes,

> Without a sense of the inherent sacredness of the
> world—of every tiny bit of life and death—we
> struggle to see God in our own reality, let alone
> to respect reality, protect it, or love it. The conse-
> quences of this ignorance are all around us, seen
> in the way we have exploited and damaged our
> fellow human beings, the dear animals, the web
> of growing things, the land, the waters, and the
> very air. (page 18)

What difference would it make to the quality of
our lives, I wonder, if we spent a little more time in
nature? Would paying attention to the life cycles of

animals or the annual changes of landscapes give us an increased sense of respect for the environment? How would eating seasonal local food affect our patterns of consumption and our health and well-being? Ordinary experiences of nature, like these moments out on the water, can renew our sense of reverence and remind us of how deeply interconnected we all are.

As I return down the length of the bay, the sun sets, streaming pink hues across the darkening sky. The sheep in the solitary green field saunter down toward the cliff edge to take their place for the night. As the wavelets lap over my feet, the gentle breeze softens to a whisper. I take a deep breath of cold air and feel my body relax. I'm in heaven.

REFLECTIVE EXERCISES

Spend some time in nature, ideally somewhere you can encounter at least one animal. This could be any of the following places:

• in a garden
• in a field
• in a forest
• by the coast

Go anywhere that feels wild and alive. (If this is difficult for you to do, watch a video clip of your favorite landscapes or wildlife footage.)

1. At some point during your time in nature, quiet your body and pay attention to the beauty, the complexity, and the sacredness of this landscape and any animals with which you share this space.

2. Reflect on how God is revealed to you through this first Incarnation. Journal what this evokes within you.

Personal and Universal: The Second Incarnation

Right now, perhaps more than ever, we need a God as big as the still-expanding universe, or educated people will continue to think of God as a mere add-on to a world that is already awesome, beautiful, and worthy of praise in itself. If Jesus is not also presented as Christ, I predict more and more people will not so much actively rebel against Christianity as just gradually lose interest in it. (page 17)

A t some point in my childhood, or at least during my study of theology, I wish somebody would have clearly explained to me that *"Christ is God, and Jesus is the Christ's historical manifestation in time"* (page 19).

It's so simple and yet so profound. Instead of reflecting on this sublime distinction, many of us merely confuse the names Jesus and Christ, often using them interchangeably.

In the 1990s, Rowan Atkinson co-wrote and starred in the famous British sitcom *Mr. Bean*. The show's opening sequence begins with some very beautiful choral singing in Latin, and then a beam of light appears from above, as if from a spaceship. The beam widens into a full circle on the cobblestone street, and a fully grown man, Mr. Bean, is beamed down as if visiting us from space. When I was younger, I wondered if this might have been similar to how Jesus arrived to visit us. Was he beamed down from heaven, an alien God coming to live with us for a few years? Fr. Richard writes that the reality is the exact opposite:

> Instead of saying that God came *into* the world through Jesus, maybe it would be better to say that Jesus came *out of* an already Christ-soaked world. The second Incarnation flowed out of the first, out of God's loving union with physical creation. (page 15)

This is no visitation from *another* world. God's presence is a revelation—quite literally a revealing or an uncovering—from *within* this world. When we breathe in the fresh air, swim in the sea, walk in a forest, touch the soil with our bare feet, and interact with animals and other humans, we are solidly connected to the first Incarnation. Then the second Incarnation emerges from within the first. But it can be difficult for us to resonate with both the personal and the universal aspect of this second Incarnation in equal measure.

The sound of the hard Greek *ch* has always made the word *Christ* seem formal and somewhat distant to me. During Mass at our high school chapel, the most solemn prayers ended, "Through Christ our Lord. Amen." Bells would ring, incense would burn, and the mighty Christ figure remained far removed. How could the man Jesus be the same person? He had picnics with his friends, he was kind and compassionate, he was a bit of a wanderer and an adventurer, and apparently he was good with his hands. It just wouldn't make sense to end a prayer with, "Through Jesus our Lord. Amen."

But at college, I learned that many of my friends from different backgrounds ended prayers with, "In Jesus's name. Amen." I learned that some people are very comfortable praying directly to Jesus in quite an informal way. The word *Christ* barely got a mention.

One Christmas, I brought one of my friends to midnight Mass at my old high school. He had never seen such ceremony or heard a small orchestra perform in church. He now saw why I struggled with the more informal Jesus-centric services I had attended with him. As we discussed it afterward, I realized that my upbringing and personality influenced me to connect much more with the universal than the personal aspect of the second Incarnation. My friend's faith upbringing was quite the opposite; it was very relaxed and informal. But he appreciated the symbolism of this midnight Mass: how the congregation processed past an open fire on the way into the darkness of the silent chapel, the huge choir singing old hymns in different languages. He could sense the awe and wonder of Christ in this ceremony. It was enlightening for us both.

Fr. Richard writes that we need both the personal and universal expressions of Christ:

A merely personal God becomes tribal and sentimental, and a merely universal God never leaves the realm of abstract theory and philosophical principles. . . . To be loved by Jesus enlarges our heart capacity. To be loved by the Christ enlarges our *mental* capacity. We need both a Jesus and a Christ, in my opinion, to get the full picture. A truly transformative God—for both the individual and history—needs to be experienced as both personal and universal. (pages 19, 36)

REFLECTIVE EXERCISES

1. With which aspect of the second Incarnation do you most resonate: the personal (Jesus) or the universal (Christ)?

2. Write a prayer or a letter to the person of God the Son that you're not as familiar with, either Jesus or the Christ. You may have questions to ask. Perhaps you have a desire for deeper connection and intimacy with Christ. Perhaps you are confused by the idea of Jesus emerging from within a Christ-soaked world. Don't overthink it; just start writing and see what comes up for you.

Becoming

God loves things by becoming them.
God loves things by uniting with them, not by excluding
them. (page 16)

In his book *Immortal Diamond: The Search for Our True Self,* Fr. Richard writes extensively about the human struggle to more fully embrace who "you are in God."[1] He calls this your *True Self,* your "absolute identity," where you become conscious that "you are in God" and "God is in you."[2] The first step to embracing your *True Self* is to become aware of and accept your *False Self.*

The *False Self* is your "needy and fragile" self.[3] It's who you think you are based on the identities we are initially drawn to in life: roles such as a parent, a partner, or a helpful friend, and respected titles such as a doctor, a leader, or a pastor. There is nothing wrong with or bad about your *False Self;* it's simply "the identity you created for yourself," "the illusion that must pass" so that you can mature and become more fully the person God made you to be.[4]

Using slightly different language, the author and social researcher Brené Brown talks about the importance of facing areas of vulnerability, fear, and even shame in our lives. She writes, "Owning our story and loving ourselves through that process is the bravest thing that we will ever do."[5] This means that the path of becoming fully human, the road toward our *True Self,* requires us to be honest about our most challenging experiences: how we love and respect our bodies, how we deal with the pain of the loss of a loved one, how we embrace a crisis of faith, how we acknowledge struggles with our sexuality or the heartbreak of rejection. Even simple things like failing an exam, losing in sports, or not having the courage to speak up and give our opinion can significantly affect our self-image.

In essence, we need to embrace a holistic perspective of life that has space for all our experiences, both the identities that we cling to and the vulnerabilities that we hide. Fr. Richard writes,

> What I am calling in this book an *incarnational worldview* is the profound recognition of the pres-

ence of the divine in literally "every thing" and "every one." It is the key to mental and spiritual health, as well as to a kind of basic contentment and happiness. An incarnational worldview is the only way we can reconcile our inner worlds with the outer one, unity with diversity, physical with spiritual, individual with corporate, and divine with human. (page 18)

If you are anything like me, you know how easy it is to hide behind one identity or another, thinking it will make us look good. Some of us pursue success, hiding behind more and more achievements. Others pursue perfection, seeking control at all costs in order to feel safe and secure. Being an expert on a subject, belonging to the in-group, being a creative or a free spirit—these are all examples of good identities with which we can easily overidentify. Yet they are "illusions that must pass," writes Fr. Richard.[6]

Whenever we hide behind these identities in order to bury our vulnerabilities, our shame, or our fear, we stop maturing into the whole people God made us to be. Fr. Richard reminds us that "*God loves things by uniting with them, not by excluding them*" (page 16). In the same way, we, too, need to accept and include all the aspects of ourselves—even those aspects we'd prefer to exclude. Only then can we become whole people, our *True Selves.* This is challenging and often frightening, and we tend not to go there until we absolutely have to.

Which parts of yourself would you prefer to exclude? Was there a key moment or experience that led you to begin to face this? Perhaps it's still to come.

> *Jesus came to show us how to be human much more than how to be spiritual,* and the process still seems to be in its early stages. (page 23)

REFLECTIVE EXERCISES

1. What aspects of your life do you tend to ignore or exclude? What experiences, stories, and opinions do you tend to shy away from, even though they are truly a part of who God made you to be?

2. What identities have you constructed that protect you from showing areas of vulnerability or fear or shame to yourself and others? Reflect for a moment on the energy you expend in order to maintain these identities.

3. Notice what's coming to mind as you read these questions. You may want to pray or journal about the process of becoming more of who God made you to be, your *True Self.*

The Path Toward Inner Aliveness

Faith at its essential core is *accepting that we are accepted!* We cannot deeply know ourselves without also knowing the One who made us, and we cannot fully accept ourselves without accepting God's radical acceptance of every part of us. (page 29)

Paying too much attention to the voices of others is one of the biggest challenges that keeps us from "accepting that we are accepted," Fr. Richard writes (page 29). We are social beings, and we need to learn from one another. But if we spend too much time looking outside ourselves for affirmation, we can lose touch with who we're made to be, our *True Self.*

From the time of the Industrial Revolution onward, the Western world has embraced the metaphor of the machine. We take an idea like Newton's third law of motion ("For every action there is an equal and opposite reaction") and unconsciously apply it to our lives. "What will happen if I take this step? How do I know I'll definitely get what I'm looking for?" This often leads us to dualistic thinking, in which we attempt to study the complexity of our lives in the same way we would examine a machine. "What are the ten steps I need to take to have a successful relationship? What are the five tips to consider in getting ahead in my career? What one thing does God require me to do next?" A machine can be studied and understood, with its inputs, throughputs, and outputs. But it's too narrow a metaphor for the expansiveness of life.

When Fr. Richard writes, "How you get there is where you arrive," he is gently inviting us to shift our focus from mechanistic outcomes to the moment-by-moment experiences of life itself (page 29). It takes time and practice for this to happen. We need contemplative practices that invite us into new ways of thinking and seeing, and we also need a bigger vision of what this kind of life could look like.

"In my opinion," Fr. Richard writes, "[Jesus's] aliveness made it so much easier for people to trust their own aliveness and thus relate to God, because *like knows like*" (page 33). This has been my experience. As a young boy, I was frequently asked what I wanted to do when I grew up. I didn't know. But adults asked me so much that I started thinking about the future, and I began to create plans based on what others told me was good. I became skilled at giving adults the answers they wanted to hear, and I slowly started to convince myself that I wanted these things too.

My guidance counselor in high school, upon hearing my career plans, wisely quoted Thomas Merton to me: "People may spend their whole lives climbing the ladder of success only to find, once they reach the top, that the ladder is leaning against the wrong wall."[1] She could see that I wasn't accepting of myself, that I was making decisions based on scarcity and fear. I wasn't ready to begin to trust my own inner aliveness and really listen.

Instead of asking, "What do you want to do when you grow up?," a better question would have been, "Who do you want to be?" Better still, "*How* do you want to be?" What kind of presence do you want to bring to this world?

Fr. Richard asks a question that highlights our struggle to trust ourselves and accept who Jesus says we are:

> Have you ever noticed that the expression "the light of the world" is used to describe the Christ (John 8:12), but that Jesus also applies the same

phrase to us? (Matthew 5:14, "You are the light of the world.") Few preachers ever pointed that out to me. (page 31)

As we connect with our interior world, with what's really motivating our life choices and our behavior, sometimes we have to accept that we do not "trust [our] own aliveness" (page 33) and we do not believe Jesus when he says that "[we] are the light of the world." We are so focused on external affirmation, doing things for the benefit of others, that we end up hiding the light (Luke 8:16) of our *True Self*.

REFLECTIVE EXERCISES

1. Take five minutes to silently reflect on significant decisions you have made in your life. This could be anything from a career choice to a relationship, from choosing your closest friends to deciding where to live.
2. In making these decisions, were you more influenced by the expectations of others or by your own inner aliveness?
3. Write a journal entry about your sense of connection to your inner aliveness today. Notice the emotions and sensations that this journaling exercise evokes.

Reflection 10

Including

The sacramental principle is this: *Begin with a concrete moment of encounter, based in this physical world, and the soul universalizes from there, so that what is true here becomes true everywhere else too.* And so the spiritual journey proceeds with ever-greater circles of inclusion into the One Holy Mystery! (page 31)

We live in a world where, for ease of understanding, we regularly divide things into what's in and what's out, what's included and what's excluded. The more time we spend viewing the world from this perspective, the more likely we are to apply it to ourselves. Which parts of me are "good" and worthy of expression? Which parts are shameful and "bad"? What can I safely reveal to others, and what do I need to hide?

Most of us spend our teenage years trying to answer these questions, inventing and reinventing ourselves by way of the friends we have and the things we do. This pattern means that we often define ourselves by what we *are not* long before we see and accept who we really are. This can go on for many decades as we continue to look outside ourselves for our sense of identity. And it's easy to bring this into our experience of faith, judging others who are different from us on grounds of belief and behavior.

Fr. Richard writes that one sign of growth and maturity on our spiritual journeys is that we proceed "with ever-greater circles of inclusion" (page 31). One day, you come to the point where you realize, *"You are not your gender, your nationality, your ethnicity, your skin color, or your social class. . . . You are a child of God, and always will be, even when you don't believe it"* (pages 36–37). But so many of our faith experiences, our church's doctrinal documents, and our community's attitudes seem to point in the opposite direction. To those who argue that making distinctions and highlighting difference is fundamental to the Christian faith, Fr. Richard writes, "The only people that Jesus seemed to exclude were precisely those who refused to know they were ordinary sinners like everyone else. *The only thing he excluded was exclusion itself*" (page 34).

To escape this pattern of including some and excluding others, we need to acknowledge what's really going on within ourselves. In psychological terms, one of the many reasons we continue to judge others, even when we are trying not to, is because we are engaging in projection. We turn a blind eye toward characteristics within our personality that don't fit our idealized self-image, but when we see others display these same characteristics, we have a strong reaction toward them. What's happening when we project is that we are refusing to address those parts of ourselves that we struggle to accept. We don't want to face them, and we become outraged when others put them on display.

There is no easy way through this pattern of including and excluding. It's our life's work. But the sooner we acknowledge it and the deeper we go in addressing it, the greater the chance that things can change within and that we can see Christ "in those who *do not like* [us], and those who *are not like* [us]" (page 37). Even more, you might begin to really hear and trust that *"you are a child of God, and always will be, even when you don't believe it"* (page 37).

REFLECTIVE EXERCISES

1. Think of a time when you excluded an individual because of something you disliked about them. (For example, they tended to be late or they dominated conversation.) How did this experience of exclusion affect the other person? How did your excluding them affect you?

2. In what ways have you felt included by others? Choose a specific example and journal as many details as you can remember—not only what happened but also how it made you feel and how it affected you beyond the initial moment of inclusion.

3. As you reflect on these moments of exclusion and inclusion, consider responding, as Fr. Richard writes, with a "concrete moment of encounter" (page 31). Trust your gut instinct and let your intuition guide you. You may select a number of responses, beyond the examples listed below:

• If you had a lot of thoughts and insights reading this reflection, you might write them down in your journal.

• If you feel emotionally upset in any way, perhaps listen to your favorite music or go for a calming walk in nature to restore your sense of peace.

• If you feel like you want to reconnect with someone, make contact with that old friend or acquaintance.

• If you need some support or guidance, talk to a family member, a trusted friend, or a helping professional (for example, a counselor).

Reflection 11

Our Own Human Experience

Paul, like us, never knew Jesus in the flesh. Like him, we only know the Christ through observing and honoring the depth of our own human experience. (page 42)

I once had the opportunity to visit several of the coastal sites where Jesus taught around the Sea of Galilee. A combination of my own excitement and the sweltering heat meant that I struggled to sleep in our tent. So I walked the beach, looked across the lake at the lights of Tiberias, lay down on the warm sand, and gazed up at the stars. How amazing it would have been to meet Jesus in the flesh, I thought. To go on a night fishing trip there with him and his friends. It would be so much easier to connect with him if I had met him in person.

But even Paul never got to meet Jesus in the flesh. Instead, he had to rely on an unfolding inner awareness of the Christ for his spiritual transformation. Fr. Richard writes that this huge shift in Paul's life—this moving from one way of seeing the world to a very different way, through encountering the Christ—is available to us all. In fact, Paul's story is the "archetypal spiritual pattern, wherein people move *from what they thought they always knew to what they now fully recognize*" (page 40).

The path for us to know the Christ in this powerful way, continues Fr. Richard, is "through observing and honoring the depth of our own human experience" (page 42). For some of us, this is an exciting prospect, one that we are used to and desire to pursue. But for others, this can seem quite daunting.

When we read a statement like, "*I have never been separate from God, nor can I be, except in my mind,*" some of us might find that it resonates with our whole being (page 44). For others, we detect a defensiveness rising up from within, telling us, *That's not right,* or asking, *Am I allowed to think that way?* Regardless of our background, religious or not, if we have spent a lot of time in environments that don't value the exploration of different perspectives, a new idea can seem like a potential threat.

Some of Fr. Richard's words and the reflective exercises in this book will likely evoke emotions that we would prefer to suppress. We may even experience physical sensations, such as a sinking feeling or shortness of breath, which are our bodies' way of telling us that it doesn't feel safe. If this is the case, we need to be kind to ourselves and to proceed gently. From my personal experiences, as well as my work, I know that meaningful and healthy inner change takes place in environments where we feel very safe and secure.

As you continue to read this book, I encourage you to pay attention to your reactions to the quotations and the reflective exercises. Observe and honor "the depth of [your] own human experience." Notice what you shy away from. Notice what resonates. Continue to remind yourself, "*I have never been separate from God, nor can I be, except in my mind*" (page 44).

REFLECTIVE EXERCISES

Take a few moments to read this quotation two or three times:

> *En Cristo* seems to be Paul's code word for *the gracious, participatory experience of salvation,* the path that he so urgently wanted to share with the world. Succinctly put, this identity means *humanity has never been separate from God*—unless and except by its own negative choice. All of us, without exception, are living inside of a cosmic identity, already in place, that is driving and guiding us forward. We are all *en Cristo,* willingly or unwill-

ingly, happily or unhappily, consciously or unconsciously. (page 43)

Now pause and reflect.

1. What words most stood out to you? Take a minute to write these down.

2. What emotions did you feel? Possibilities include relief at the realization that you have never been separate from God, frustration at how this message clashes with what you believe. You don't have to understand why you felt these emotions, just pay attention to them and take note of them.

3. What physical sensations, if any, were you aware of as you read or sat with this quotation? Simply pay attention to them and record them for yourself.

4. Finally, take a few moments to journal anything that is coming to mind for you right now—either related to the questions above or something entirely different.

Image, Love, and Suffering

You tend to create a God who is just like you—whereas it was supposed to be the other way around. . . . God hardly ever holds on to control, if the truth be told. . . . Any kind of authentic God experience will usually feel like love or suffering, or both.
(page 51)

Movies and popular culture have given us many examples of religious people who "create a God who is just like" them. Some are beautiful examples, like the wise and caring Fr. Gabriel in the movie *The Mission* (1986) or the devout and principled athlete, Eric Liddell, in *Chariots of Fire* (1981). But many other examples reflect an image of a God who wants to stay firmly in control, regardless of how negatively this affects others. These include the moralizing Reverend Moore in *Footloose* (1984) and Hilary Faye Stockard in the satirical comedy *Saved!* (2004). In one scene, Hilary Faye's friend accuses her of not knowing "the first thing about love." Hilary responds with rage, screams that she is *filled* with Christ's love, and proceeds to throw a Bible at her friend.

The connotations that come to mind when we hear the words "God" and "Jesus Christ" are directly related to our experiences of Christianity within our culture and our immediate community. In chapter 6, Fr. Richard considers how Carl Jung's observations of his father and uncles, who were all ministers, inspired him to move away from their take on Christianity, as they all seemed "to be unhappy and unhealthy men" (page 84). But Fr. Richard's own experiences of the Irish nuns and priests who taught and ministered to him as a little boy left him with a totally different, very positive impression. Our view of God often depends on what has been modeled for us in our culture and community and on the depth of connection we feel toward these role models.

Fr. Richard tells us that "the Christ, especially when twinned with Jesus, is a clear message about *universal love and necessary suffering as the divine pattern*" (page 50). In Jesus Christ, God models the giving of great love, the letting go of control, and the allowing of great suffering so as to create something new. This is just like the pattern of spiritual transformation (Reflection 2), which describes the archetypical manner in which we experience universal love and necessary suffering over time.

Fr. Richard writes that this pattern is rooted in "the three persons of the Trinity, where *God is said to be both endlessly outpouring and self-emptying*. Like three revolving buckets on a waterwheel, this process keeps the Flow flowing eternally—inside and outside of God, and in one positive direction" (pages 50–51).

Some of us gave up on God or Christianity because we never expected the self-emptying part of the water-wheel. We didn't sign up for "necessary suffering," and we weren't prepared for a deep loss of control. I remember a church history lecturer explaining that in the first few centuries CE, it could take up to three years of preparation to be baptized as a Christian. The early church leaders wanted to make sure that people really knew what they were signing up for: a path of descent and letting go. You are baptized into your death.

But in the absence of this message being clearly communicated, our experiences of bereavement, illness, breakups, loneliness, and loss of friends and work can all lead us to question our faith. And if we surround ourselves with people and environments that focus only on overcoming, resurrection, and the positive upsides of reorder, it's hard to see any place for suffering in our spirituality or our ideal plan for our lives. But Fr. Richard reminds us that experiences of loss and suffering are one of the two major pathways that God uses to draw us toward deeper intimacy and maturity.

> Only great love and great suffering are strong enough to take away our imperial ego's protections and open us to authentic experiences of transcendence. (page 50)

REFLECTIVE EXERCISES

Fr. Richard writes,

> Our circles of belonging tend to either expand or constrict as life goes on. . . . Our patterns of relating, once set, determine the trajectories for our whole lives. If we are inherently skeptical and suspicious, the focus narrows. If we are hopeful and trusting, the focus continues to expand. (page 51)

1. What words would you use to describe your image of God?
2. In what ways has this image been modeled by others around you?
3. Would others characterize you as someone whose "circles of belonging" are expanding or constricting as your "life goes on"?

Reflection 13

Primal Goodness

Most of the world's great religions start with some sense of primal goodness in their creation stories. The Judeo-Christian tradition beautifully succeeded at this, with the Genesis record telling us that God called creation "good" five times in Genesis 1:10–25, and even "very good" in 1:31. . . . After Augustine, most Christian theologies shifted from the positive vision of Genesis 1 to the darker vision of Genesis 3—the so-called fall, or what I am calling the "problem." Instead of embracing God's master plan for humanity and creation . . . Christians shrunk our image of both Jesus and Christ, and our "Savior" became a mere Johnny-come-lately "answer" to the problem of sin, a problem that we had largely created ourselves. (pages 61–62)

In my teens, the terror of original sin weighed heavily on me. It was linked to my poor self-image, my legalistic upbringing, and the idea, taken from Genesis 3 and the writings of St. Augustine, that humans are fallen and troubled by nature. I walked away from my faith, as I simply couldn't live up to the standards of behavior it seemed to demand. Plus, I couldn't see how the love, joy, and peace mentioned at Mass were connected to my daily experiences of shifting friendships, family challenges, and the pressures of school and competitive sport. It was only when I went on my final high school retreat with our school chaplain that I really began to understand how a person of faith could live from an alternative perspective to the sin-focused Genesis 3 outlook on life.

Fr. Frank embodied a world-affirming Genesis 1 perspective. He saw all people as good, all creativity as emanating from the Divine, and all our best intentions to be the Holy Spirit's invitation into deeper intimacy with a God who loves us completely. In his understanding, there were no ifs, buts, or conditions of any kind to God's love. It was a staggering shift in outlook for me, one that I questioned and argued against time and again as I slowly let go of my fear-based view of God and my accompanying negative self-image. It took lots of reading and discussions with Fr. Frank for me to move from a Genesis 3 focus on sin to a Genesis 1 outlook on primal goodness.

Over the years of our friendship, I learned how this slight, quiet man in his seventies had gone up against bishops and archbishops, defending the LGBTQ community within the church, promoting the deeper inclusion of refugees, and asking those in power to engage as equitably with the poor as with the rich. He modeled for me the good and loving way that God engages with us.

One evening, after another prolonged barrage of my theological questions, Fr. Frank laughed and said, "I haven't gone into this much detail since seminary! Theology is important, but spirituality is far more important. That will stay with you your whole life." Something clicked for me that evening. Over the following years, I began to explore practices that could help me embody my evolving theological beliefs: from sitting contemplatively to walking a labyrinth; from making quarterly retreats to journaling to engaging in acts of service. I moved from solely emphasizing the intellectual aspects of theology to a more holistic approach to everyday life and spirituality.

Even today, decades after our childhoods, some of my close friends still struggle to accept that they are fundamentally good and eternally lovable. For some, it has led them to reject their faith outright. The emphasis on sin in their faith communities produced more shame and guilt than they could bear.

In stark contrast, Fr. Richard beautifully reminds us,

The initial metaphor for creation was a garden, which is inherently positive, beautiful, growth-oriented, a place to be "cultivated and cared for" (Genesis 2:15), where humans could walk naked and without shame. (page 61)

I wonder what difference it would make in our own lives, within our communities and across our whole society, if we could more fully embrace this beautiful vision. We might experience more of God's primal goodness, both within ourselves and in the world around us.

REFLECTIVE EXERCISES

1. Describe God from a Genesis 3 and a Genesis 1 worldview. Resist overthinking and trust your intuition when answering this.

GENESIS 3—focused on the fall and the problem of sin	GENESIS 1—focused on primal goodness, where humans can live without shame
• E.g. God demands perfection of me	• E.g. God believes in me and trusts my good intentions, even when I live from a place of fear or judgment

2. How have you experienced each of these worldviews in your daily life? In what ways have they affected your self-image and your perceptions of others? Resist over-thinking and trust your intuition when answering this.

GENESIS 3—focused on the fall and the problem of sin	GENESIS 1—focused on primal goodness, where humans can live without shame
• E.g. I demand perfection from those around me	• E.g. I trust the good intentions in strangers I meet, even when they seem difficult

As you reflect on what you wrote, notice any desires that you have for the future. You may find it helpful to pray about or journal your response.

Reflection 14

The Great Chain of Being

To work up to loving God, start by loving the very humblest and simplest things. . . . Don't start by trying to love God, or even people; love rocks and elements first, move to trees, then animals, and then humans. . . . It might be the only way to love, because *how you do anything is how you do everything.* (page 57)

Drawing on the work of St. Bonaventure and others, Fr. Richard beautifully expresses this medieval notion of connecting with God through the "Great Chain of Being." These medieval mystics were intuiting what recent research has revealed: that our brains and bodies are wired to experience awe from nature, art, and music in particular.[1] Think of a time when your experience of a rocky landscape, a windswept forest, or an interaction with animals or people helped you feel grounded and connected to the world. Perhaps there was a moment when a piece of music, a live performance, or a work of art inspired you to stop what you were doing and become fully present to beauty, to yourself. What effect did this have?

As beautiful as these experiences are, seeking connection with God in these humble and simple moments can seem almost heretical to those who come from backgrounds that primarily value intellectual beliefs, theological explanations, and conformity with the group as marks of true spirituality.

My early days of reading the Bible led me toward such a contracted worldview that I barely allowed myself to experience God through this Great Chain of Being. Wonderful experiences of nature, art, and human kindness were nice to have, but I sidelined them in favor of theology and beliefs, which I considered to be of far more importance. Looking back, I realize that I needed permission—to know that it was okay—to experience a sense of wonder and awe for God in rocks, trees, animals, and other people.

This all came together for me the first time I was invited to go sailing. I was sent to the front of the boat, where I dangled my legs over the bow into the oncoming waves. The exhilaration of the boat's movement, the sound of the wind, and the salty spray all made me feel utterly alive and in love with the world. Then the dolphins arrived. I could see their inquisitive eyes as they swam and jumped and looked up at me. *This is magical!* I thought. *God is in all of this!* From that point onward, the links of the Great Chain continued to connect every thing together for me.

Have you ever had a similar experience, where you found yourself unexpectedly connecting with humble and simple life experiences that led you to a deeper sense of reverence and love for God?

Many of us spend most of our time feeling *disconnected* from the Great Chain of Being. We're so preoccupied with daily worries and chronic busyness that we can go hours, weeks, or even months without seeing God in the tiniest links of the chain. But eventually, a piece of music, a swim in the sea, the majesty of an ancient oak tree, or the warmth of a friend will awaken us to the "whole sacred universe" that's right here, available in each moment (page 58). Our love for God moves from the confines of theology to recognizing the Presence in *"the very humblest and simplest things"* (page 57).

REFLECTIVE EXERCISES

Anything that draws you out of yourself in a positive way—for all practical purposes—is operating as God for you at that moment. How else can the journey begin? How else are you drawn forward, now not by idle beliefs but by inner aliveness? God needs something to seduce you out and beyond yourself, so God uses three things in particular: goodness, truth, and beauty. All three have the capacity to draw us into an experience of union. (page 52)

1. Remember a time when a link of the chain helped you see the "whole sacred universe" (page 58). It could have been the goodness of another person that really inspired you or something you read, heard, or watched whose truth brought a deep resonance to your soul. Perhaps it was a beautiful piece of art or music or literature or any experience of nature that filled you with wonder.

2. Journal about how this experience affected you. How it drew *"you out of yourself"* (page 52) to love.

Waking Up to Love

Mere obedience is far too often a detour around actual love. Obedience is usually about cleaning up, love is about waking up. (page 73)

F r. Richard writes that "early-stage religion tends to focus on cleaning up, which is to say, determining who meets the requirements for moral behavior and religious belief" (page 72). Engaging with God in this way can express a beautiful intention to honor and respect all that is sacred and to walk a different path than we've walked before. After encountering the Divine, we may desire to make big changes in our behavior and our lifestyle. But there can sometimes be a sense of obligation at the heart of this focus on cleaning up.

Although some may never experience any sense of

obligation, others might think, *I need to serve in the local community in order to be a Christian* or *I have to show that I'm a good person now.* This applies as much to young children on their best behavior in church as to adults who feel duty bound to pray and obey in an acceptable way. Feelings of guilt, regret, fear, or a sense of duty can cause both children and adults to feel unlovable *unless* they clean up and behave in expected ways. It's a natural step on the path toward spiritual maturity, but it is only the first step.

In chapter 5, "Love Is the Meaning," Fr. Richard writes about the next step on that journey:

> Once you *wake up,* as Jesus and Pope Francis have, you know that cleaning up is a constant process that comes on different timetables for different people, around many different issues, and for very different motivations. This is why love and growth demand discernment, not enforcement. When it comes to actual soul work, most at-tempts at policing and conforming are largely useless. (page 73)

Like all movements in our spiritual lives, the transi-tion from cleaning up to waking up can be elusive to pin down. We may experience it as a "loosening of the screws," an easing up of some of the rules we've worked hard to follow, while being simultaneously drawn into a deeper experience of great love. As we navigate this journey, Fr. Richard reminds us that "*God loves you by becoming you,* taking your side in the inner dialogue of self-accusation and defense," unfolding "your person-hood from within through a *constant increase in freedom*" (page 79).

This growing sense of freedom is a pivotal sign that we are waking up. But it doesn't just come about through some kind of monastic level of introspection. "Most humans," according to Fr. Richard, "need a love object": "someone or something to connect our hearts with our heads" (page 74). We need something to draw us out of ourselves, away from the rituals and rules of cleaning up into a bigger story of giving and receiving deep love.

We might have the same singular love object that lasts the span of our entire lives, or we may experience a multiplicity of love objects over the years. I have known friends whose diversity of love objects have ranged from the study of history to the love of their dog, from the community of online gaming to serving as a doctor in war zones around the globe. Their deep love for each of these "North Stars" grounded them "by creating focus, direction, motivation, even joy," sometimes when little else in life did (page 74).

For me, the first experience of a love object was in reading the Bible during my late teens. Every time I read a new passage, I felt alive, connected, focused, and included in something greater than myself. Several years later, my study of the Italian language and culture developed into another love object for me. I could feel God's beauty in every espresso I sipped in the sunlit piazza, every glass of wine I had with friends by the lake, and every opera song I heard while I lived in Verona. In time, my wife became my primary love object. As we dated and later married, supporting her and making her a priority for my time and energy became a deeply transformative experience. Her love for me deepened my sense of security and self-confidence, drawing me out of myself toward loving her even more. Now, as we begin to feel the kicks of our first child, we both have an intuition that our baby will become the next significant love object that connects us to God's ever-unfolding love.

Our need for "a love object (which will then become a subject!)," writes Fr. Richard, is a representation of "the God Instinct, which we might just call the 'need to adore'" (page 74). As Rumi, the Sufi poet and mystic, put it, "We need at least one place where we can 'kneel and kiss the ground'"[1] (page 74).

REFLECTIVE EXERCISES

As I look at the things and people I have tried to love in my life, I would have to say, "They made me do it!" It was the inherent goodness, inner beauty, vulnerability, deep honesty, or generosity of spirit from the other side that drew me out of myself and toward them. (page 77)

1. Who or what has been a love object for you in the past?

2. Who or what is a love object for you today?

3. Journal about an experience when a love object drew out beauty, goodness, or love in you.

Suffering

Christ [is] a universally available "voice" that calls all things to *become whole and true to themselves.* God's two main tools in this direction, from every appearance, seem to be great love and great suffering—and often great love that *invariably leads* to great suffering. (page 83)

M ost of us regularly experience some degree of suffering: from breakdowns in relationships to career disappointments, from financial struggles to health problems and significant trauma. In addition to these pains of everyday life, many also experience racism, sexism, ageism, and the countless other injustices that are, unfortunately, common in most of our communities today.

In a society whose overarching narrative is that we are entitled to be happy, to pursue pleasure, and to enjoy success, it can be confusing to know what to do with our suffering. In many cases, people's pain is compounded by society's downplaying, or even denying, that such suffering exists. Fr. Richard writes that at some point, we need to acknowledge our suffering, sit with it, and allow Christ's "universally available 'voice'" to speak from within our pain.

> The supreme irony of life is that this voice of Christ works through . . . what always seems like unwholeness and untruth! God insists on incorporating the seeming negative. There is no doubt that God allows suffering. In fact, *God seems to send us on the path toward our own wholeness not by eliminating the obstacles, but by making use of them.* (page 83)

My experience of depression as a teenager led me to the very edge of myself and almost beyond. I internalized the messages I received from experiences of disappointment and difficult relationships, culminating in a deep dislike for myself. I considered my life to be utterly pointless. It took many years of healing just to *begin* to be comfortable with who I was.

Fr. Richard writes about how the author Etty Hillesum integrated her sensual and spiritual experi-

ences amid great suffering in World War II. Despite the
fact that she was interred, and subsequently died, in a
concentration camp, her final years of writing give as-
tonishing insight into her intimacy with God and her
deep resonance within herself. Etty's ability to experience love objects and the beauty of the first Incarnation
amid her own suffering is an example of what St. Bonaventure called the "coincidence of opposites" (page
83): the ability to hold the tension of suffering and love
in one's daily experience.

It's so tempting to get rid of, to avoid, or to numb
our suffering. It can take quite a while to accept that it
is part of life and that being present to it is the most
realistic and honest way of living. But once we stop trying to resolve our pain and start sitting with our suffering, we can really listen to what it has to teach us. Over
time, we may even experience moments of hope and
flashes of freedom. Our pain or our sense of injustice
can grow into something much bigger, something
transformational. As we face our pain, we are better
placed to help victims, perpetrators, and entire systems
face theirs.

STAYING WITHIN YOUR COMFORT ZONE WHILE
REFLECTING ON PERSONAL SUFFERING[1]

Many of us have unhealed pain or trauma that might be
triggered by these reflections on suffering. This pain or
trauma could be from a childhood experience or more

recent events. It might be something of which you are fully aware, or it might be hidden in your body.

If that's true for you, it is important to adapt the following reflections or skip them completely. Take care not to push yourself beyond your comfort zone. If you experience very negative emotions or sensations (such as dizziness, rage, intense crying, hyperventilation, or disconnection from your body), please contact a mental health professional (a counselor, psychotherapist, or psychiatrist) for support.

If you feel unexpectedly triggered, please consider supporting yourself in the following ways:

• Speak aloud to yourself (for example, "It's okay. I'm okay. I am here now and safe in this moment. I'm not trapped in a past experience that wasn't so safe.").
• Stand up and walk around.
• Touch the floor, the ground, or something within reach that makes you feel safe and "at home" when you touch it (such as a piece of fabric or a small keepsake).
• Smell something that brings good memories to mind (for example, a favorite food, fragrance, or essential oil).
• Listen to a piece of music or any sound that brings you a sense of calm.
• Look at a photo of someone or something that calls to mind good memories or has positive connotations for you.

• In the absence of a photo, picture in your mind's eye an image that calls to mind good memories or has positive connotations or say it aloud (for example, "The warm sun, the blue sea, the quiet beach, the peaceful garden").

My hope is that you will feel safe as you continue to reflect throughout this book.

REFLECTIVE EXERCISES

God hides in the depths and is not seen as long as we stay on the surface of anything. . . . The archetypal encounter between doubting Thomas and the Risen Jesus (John 20:19–28) is not really a story about believing in the fact of the Resurrection, but a story about believing that someone could be wounded and also resurrected at the same time! . . . In fact, this might be the primary pastoral message of the whole Gospel. (page 111)

1. How have you tended to deal with your pain and suffering in the past (for example, avoid it, sit with it, or blame others for it)?
2. How are you right now? What emotions do you feel? What sensations do you notice in your body? Pay attention to what you need to listen to in this moment.

Reflection 17

Our Shadow

The God Archetype is the part of you that drives you toward greater inclusivity by deep acceptance of the Real, the balancing of opposites, simple compassion toward the self, and the ability to recognize and forgive your own shadow side. (page 84)

As we take the courageous step toward embracing great suffering and great love and allowing them to transform us, we inevitably encounter our shadow. In his book *Falling Upward: A Spirituality for the Two Halves of Life,* Fr. Richard defines the shadow as "what you refuse to see about yourself, and what you do not want others to see."[1] It has a drive and energy of its own that motivates us to portray idealized images of ourselves to the world. An idealized image, which Jung called a persona,[2] allows us to be seen in ways that are rewarded by others and make us feel good about ourselves.

Fr. Richard writes:

> Be especially careful therefore of any idealized role or self-image, like that of minister, mother, doctor, nice person, professor, moral believer, or president of this or that. These are huge personas to live up to, and they trap many people in life-long delusion. The more you are attached to and unaware of such a protected self-image, the more shadow self you will very likely have.[3]

Growing up, I developed a persona of someone who was organized and focused in getting any job done. This way of being helped me survive my very demanding and stressful childhood. When I entered the workplace, others began to comment on my busy lifestyle and the amount of activities I completed each day. Working with colleagues and teams, I pushed for a fast pace and a clear path toward achieving big goals. But one thing I couldn't abide was working with people who were consistently inefficient or disorganized.

As I grew in my responsibilities, I became known as a person who was successful at working with leaders and teams (my efficient, effective persona). Unbeknown to me, however, I was also becoming known as someone who was impatient and demanding (my shadow). All the while, I prided myself on my empathy and was convinced that I was putting people first.

It's important to remember that our shadow is the flip side of our persona—the shadow we cast as we seek to live well in the world. "The shadow self invariably presents itself as something like prudence, common sense, justice, or 'I am doing this for your good,'" Fr. Richard writes, "when it is actually manifesting fear, control, manipulation, or even vengeance."[4] This means our shadow often comes about as a by-product of our good intentions.

Yet our shadow is not our sin or something we should seek to cast off. Fr. Richard reminds us that "*the greater light you are, the greater shadow you cast*" (page 197). We need to identify this shadow, develop it, and then integrate it for our gold and our light to manifest in the world.

One way of identifying our shadow is to notice what traits frustrate us in other people. What situations provoke a reaction from us? Fr. Richard writes,

> Invariably when something upsets you, and you have a strong emotional reaction out of proportion to the moment, your shadow self has just been exposed. So watch for any overreactions or overdenials.[5]

For some of us, our shadow is weakness, and we see everyone else as needing our direction and control; for others, our shadow is anxiety, and we see others as causing stress and making a fuss. For some, our shadow is neediness, and we recoil from people who need our help. The list is endless, and the specifics of how our shadow manifests is unique to everyone. What kind of shadow do you observe within yourself?

When our shadow raises its head, we tend not to think as clearly as before. Some will feel mobilized to take action or avoid a situation (the fight-or-flight response). Others will shut down and become numb (the freeze response) or seek to ingratiate themselves with others in an attempt to move beyond relational tension (the fawn response). Over time, we might notice patterns of blaming or attacking others, retreating into ourselves, or becoming defensive. Unless we face our shadow, we will feel trapped into repeating these patterns of interpersonal dynamics, as if we are destined to experience the same thoughts and behaviors over and over again.

Identifying our shadow can take time. Asking friends and loved ones to give us honest feedback about what we are blind to requires a lot of openness and trust. But shining a light onto our shadow can lead us "toward greater inclusivity" (page 84) and a deeper sense of our True Self.[6]

REFLECTIVE EXERCISES

1. Reread this reflection a couple of times and pay close attention to your reactions. Notice any passage where you become defensive, fearful, or annoyed or feel uncomfortable in some way. Sit with these reactions for a few minutes, focusing on your thoughts, your emotions, and your bodily sensations.

2. Is there a recurring pattern to the kind of conversations you have with others or the scenarios in which you find yourself in life? For example, you might do all the tidying after others make a mess, or end up taking the lead on committees, or try your best to love others but get into arguments and regularly feel isolated or misunderstood. Is there a pattern to how your friendships and relationships tend to develop over time?

3. Take time, even a few hours or days, to reflect on these questions. You might find it helpful to ask a few trusted friends about what they see as your recurring patterns. But if you ask, be prepared for their answers; our shadows do not like being in the spotlight!

4. Write a journal entry in response to what this reflection evoked for you.

Reflection 18

Change

Jesus quite clearly believed in change. In fact, the first public word out of his mouth was the Greek imperative verb *metanoeite,* which literally translates as "change your mind" or "go beyond your mind" (Matthew 3:2; 4:17; and Mark 1:15). (page 92)

How a forgotten reality can change everything we see, hope for, and believe is a core message of *The Universal Christ.* Yet this simple concept of change is so difficult for most of us to embrace. We are creatures of habit who develop powerful patterns of thought and behavior. On a physiological level, our brain cells form neural pathways that grow stronger every time they are used. The more often we repeat a thought or action, the more normalized and embedded it becomes. It's no wonder that Jesus's opening statement in the Gospels is "Change your mind." The more attached we are to our current perspective, the more difficult any change will be.

Think of the significant life changes you've experienced and how they've influenced you. These might include becoming a parent, losing a loved one, transitioning from school to work, breaking up with a partner, embracing your sexual orientation, or falling out with a close friend. Take a moment to think of other changes you've experienced: changes to your physique and your health, moving to a new home, beginning therapy, stopping drinking, getting a promotion, leaving church, or meeting the love of your life. Reflect on your pattern of engaging with change. Is it something you welcome or something you try to avoid?

The Irish mystic, poet, and scholar John O'Donohue compared our experience of change to a baby in the womb. The baby feels safe and warm and very familiar with its environment. It has everything it needs. The sounds of the womb and the mother's heartbeat reassure the baby. But the day comes when the baby has to leave all that is familiar. Imagine the pain and the shock of slowly moving down the narrow birth canal, away from everything the baby has ever known. While everyone else celebrates a new birth, "For the baby within the womb, being born would seem like death."[1]

Fr. Richard tells us that "*resurrection and renewal are, in fact, the universal and observable pattern of everything*" (page 99) and reassures us that "God *protects us into* and *through* death, just as the Father did with Jesus" (page 93). But simply knowing that we're protected "*into* and *through* death" doesn't remove the loss that change inevitably brings. The author Mike McHargue beautifully writes about how change connects us to this "pattern of everything":

> One day, I will die, and in time my atoms will go back to giving life to something else. Much farther along the arrow of time, our own Sun will explode and spread its essence across the sky. Our Sun's dust will meet with other stars' remnants and form new stars and planets of their own. The universe itself exists in an eternal pattern of life, death, and resurrection.[2]

From the changing of the seasons to the graying of our thinning hair, change is everywhere around us. Our bodies grow rapidly throughout childhood and then complete an overhaul, renewing most cells every seven to ten years. If our muscles are not challenged, within a matter of weeks they atrophy; if our relationships are not deepening, we will eventually grow apart. Every day we have the opportunity to avoid and ignore change or to embrace it and all the possibilities it can bring.

REFLECTIVE EXERCISES

1. What kind of life changes seemed like death to you at the time but later brought about a new sense of life?

2. Has your understanding and experience of God changed over the course of your life in ways that felt significant?

3. If you're really honest with yourself, what is the next change that you need to make?

4. What needs to happen for you to "change your mind" and embrace this? Pray or journal about any thoughts or emotions this brings up for you.

Reflection 19

Up There

Most of us understandably start the journey as-
suming that God is "up there," and our job is to
transcend this world to find "him." . . . I suspect
that the "up there" mentality is the way most people's spiritual search has to start. But once the real
inner journey begins—once you come to know
that, in Christ, God is forever overcoming the gap
between human and divine—the Christian path
becomes less about climbing and performance,
and more about descending, letting go, and unlearning. (page 110)

When I visit medieval cathedrals such as the Flo-
rentine Duomo in Italy or Chartres Cathedral
in France, I'm reminded of how the architects wanted

to represent the majesty and beauty of God in the magnificence of the building. They fully expected that those who came to worship would experience a deep sense of awe. How very different these tall, spacious buildings were from the small, dark homes in which most people of the Middle Ages lived. The sheer size of Brunelleschi's dome in Florence and the light and colors of the stained-glass rose windows in Chartres continue to leave an indelible imprint on visitors today. Yet while these buildings display incredible human ingenuity and a profound sense of the Divine, they also reinforce the notion that God is "up there" somewhere and we are "down here."

My teachers at the Catholic school I attended while growing up taught me and my classmates to be on our best behavior in Mass. We had to be quiet and couldn't speak—we couldn't even smile while returning from the altar with the communion hosts in our mouths. Only when we stepped outside the chapel doors could we chat away, laugh, and be "normal" again. What a strange message to teach children. Chatting with friends, I hear of how they had to wear their Sunday best to Sunday school and sing children's worship songs about Jesus "coming down from heaven." Even our experiences of funerals, where adults point toward the sky and say the deceased is now "up there" with God, reinforce this notion that God is separate and distant. It's no wonder we struggle to believe that God is living "in here," within us.

Fr. Richard writes,

> As I watch Catholics receive communion at Mass, I notice that some, after taking the bread and wine, turn toward the altar or the sacred box that reserves the bread and bow or genuflect as a gesture of respect—as if the Presence were still over there. . . .
>
> Likewise, I have known many Evangelicals who "received Jesus into their hearts" but still felt the need to "get saved" again every Friday night. (pages 109–10)

Almost a thousand years after the construction of some of these incredible medieval cathedrals, we're still in the habit of creating dualisms in our worldview, of dividing the world into the sacred and the profane (*profanum,* meaning literally "before or outside the temple/church"). We like buildings where we can "house" God, and we like to distinguish times in our life when we can engage in "holy" activities. But when we divide the world in this way, it can cause us to spend our lives seeking experiences that give us a sense of being "up there" while burying those things that we deem to be profane.

"Throughout his life," Fr. Richard writes, "Jesus himself spent no time climbing, but a lot of time descending, *'emptying himself and becoming as all humans are'* (Philippians 2:7)" (page 110). This is so different from our tendency to push, to climb, and to develop in the hope that we will summit some sacred mountain "up there." Fr. Richard writes, "It is not insignificant that Christians chose the cross or crucifix as their central symbol," (page 216) as it is all about "unlearning, letting go, surrendering, serving others, and *not the language of self-development*" (page 217).

Imitating Jesus and emptying ourselves will look different for each one of us; we're usually aware of the things we don't want to give up. For some of us, the path of emptying might include listening to others first, seeking to understand their perspective before giving our own; choosing to contribute our gifts to a cause we care about, even if it doesn't make much money or sound very impressive to others; or accepting that life is not a checklist of events (college, career, marriage, children, and so on) that we can tick off, as there's no guarantee we'll experience all or any of these. In a society where progress, achievement, and development are championed, this self-emptying can look like madness. But the more common these small ego humiliations become, the more we tend to experience the sacred in the simplicity of the here and now.

Over time, we move beyond a dualistic view of

God being "up there" while we are "down here" to a vision where God is up there, down here, in others, and within ourselves, all at the same time. "We are all *en Cristo*" (page 43). In taking this view, we start to see that all things are sacred, including the masks we wear, the shadows we seek to hide, the wounds we carry, and the parts of ourselves we consider profane. Every thing is sacred.

REFLECTIVE EXERCISES

At one point, Jung wrote, *"My pilgrim's progress has been to climb down a thousand ladders until I could finally reach out a hand of friendship to the little clod of earth that I am"*[1] (page 86).

1. What ladders might you need to climb down to reach out a hand of friendship to yourself?
2. What tightly held beliefs or previous life experiences keep you separate from a God who seems to be "up there" instead of "in here," within you (for example, the lyrics of hymns you've sung for years or feelings of inadequacy or sinfulness every time you try to pray)?
3. What do you need to let go of, and what do you need to unlearn? Take some time to pray through or journal your response.

Reflection 20

Divine Depth

We do not need to be afraid of the depths and
breadths of our own lives, of what this world of-
fers us or asks of us. We are given permission to
become intimate with our own experiences, learn
from them, and allow ourselves to descend to the
depth of things, even our mistakes, before we try
too quickly to transcend it all in the name of some
idealized purity or superiority. (page 111)

I n this passage, Fr. Richard invites us to move away
from "disembodied spiritualities" toward a more holistic, incarnational life (page 114). But how exactly
do we do this? Fr. Richard mentions a series of helpful tools, from Integral Theory to spiritual direction
to Progoff's journaling method, that can "help us to

examine and to trust interiority and depth as never be-fore" (page 115).

In my role as a coach, consultant, and psychothera-pist, I regularly use these tools in individual and group settings. Reflecting on how to integrate them with our current self-knowledge, I like to think of the analogy of flying a small plane, where each tool represents a helpful and important dial on the dashboard. To know your altitude, you look at one dial; to know the angle of your turn, you look at another. But it's important to glance at each dial for only a moment, as none of them tell you the full picture. Of most importance is that you look out the window and fly the plane. In the same way, be present to your surroundings and live your life as it comes, consulting one or two of these tools just when needed.

Of the tools Fr. Richard mentions, the ones that have come to most prominence in recent years are the Enneagram and the Myers-Briggs Type Indicator (MBTI).[1]

The Enneagram: The Enneagram is an ancient schema that looks at nine distinct yet interconnected personality types. When I encountered it as a teenager and read the description of the Enneagram number that resonated with me, I was so amazed at its accuracy that I laughed out loud! My school chaplain, Fr. Frank, laughed too, saying, "Remember, Patrick, your num-ber is not a good thing; it's where you go for a sense of love and acceptance *instead of* going to God." The Enneagram wonderfully explains the personas we've developed that help us survive and develop in the world. Once we understand this, it can help us map a pathway toward deeper integration and wholeness, as well as love and connection with God.

MBTI: For a long time, I wondered, *What is wrong with me?* I wasn't as sociable as my peers, and I needed a lot more solo time than many others in order to reflect and rest between social interactions. The MBTI helped me understand this dynamic—that I am more introverted than extraverted—and gave me many other insights that allowed me to accept that being me is okay. Based on Carl Jung's theory of psychological types, the MBTI acknowledges that although we can behave in different ways in any setting, we do tend to have preferences that feel more natural to us.

An awareness of our MBTI type can be hugely helpful when it comes to understanding our relational dynamics with friends, the traits we're drawn to in a partner, and even our career choices. I remember when I started out as a management consultant, and a group of thirty of us plotted our MBTI types on a grid. While most were huddled into three of the sixteen possible MBTI types, I was the only person in the room whose results were plotted in the very bottom corner of the grid, away from everyone else. My perception of reality and the lenses I used to make decisions were radically different from those of my colleagues. It was no surprise that I left that role within a year.

If you know your Enneagram number and your MBTI type, take a moment to reflect on what these reveal about you, from the places you go to feel loved and accepted to the activities and environments that make you feel most at home. If you don't know your number and type, it might be worth researching the various narrative and psychometric approaches to discovering them.

As we approach the Reflective Exercises on the Enneagram and MBTI, Fr. Richard reminds us,

> Today we have freedom and permission and the tools to move toward depth as few people ever had in human history. What a shame it would be if we did not use them. (page 115)

REFLECTIVE EXERCISES

1. In what ways have your experiences of faith and spirituality encouraged and discouraged you to explore your interior life? Take some time to trace the messages you received over the course of your life—positive, negative, and everything in between—regarding the value of explorations such as these. Journal your reflections.

2. Open a book, read an article, or listen to a podcast about the Enneagram and/or the MBTI until you come to a personal insight you've not encountered before. Journal or pray about this insight and how it pertains to your lived experiences.

3. If you already have a high degree of knowledge regarding both of these tools, notice your initial reaction to the invitation to engage with this Reflective Exercise. Did it come from a place of curiosity (*I wonder what I'll learn next*), pride (*I already know all there is to know about this*), or something else entirely?

Embodying Depth

I doubt if you can see the image of God (*Imago Dei*) in your fellow humans if you cannot first see it in rudimentary form in stones, in plants and flowers, in strange little animals, in bread and wine, and most especially cannot honor this objective divine image in yourself. It is a full-body tune-up, this spiritual journey. (page 119)

If we predominantly have an intellectual understanding *of* God, more than an experiential relationship *with* God, we might be tempted to overanalyze ourselves when we engage with tools like the Enneagram and MBTI. In addition to these methods of personal reflection, human beings have spent millennia engaging in a wide range of embodied practices that help us recognize God's image and enter into the depth of things. These include body-based therapies and Fr. Richard's suggestions of wilderness training and certain kinds of embodied grief and bereavement work (page 115). Let me suggest three more you might consider: a retreat, a pilgrimage, and a labyrinth.

Retreat: Making a retreat to a deserted landscape is an ancient practice, one in which Jesus, the Desert Mothers and Fathers, and many more have participated for thousands of years. The stillness of the landscape, the natural rhythm of sunrise and sunset, the simplicity of time away from technology, and our increased awareness of animals and nature can all lead even the busiest of minds to slow down.

A retreat doesn't have to be a time-consuming affair that takes place somewhere far away. Often, a one-day or even a half-day local retreat is the only practicable approach to take. A retreat can be made alone or, as is the case in many retreat centers, as a group guided through the experience by a retreat leader. Personally, I enjoy making a retreat by myself, in a valley or by the coast. I find that keeping a journal to write down my thoughts and concerns helps me during the first few hours until, finally, I "arrive" and can pay attention to the physical nature of the environment and my body. I start to notice any tension I'm carrying, how I breathe, and whether I want to move a lot or simply catch up on sleep. I listen to myself and to God from a wholly different, interior place.

Pilgrimage: The practice of a walking pilgrimage can be an exhilarating and exhausting experience. There are so many pilgrims' paths around the world, from the famous Camino de Santiago across northern Spain to the 1,500-year-old pilgrims' paths through the Irish mountains near my home. Pilgrims often carry an intention or make a prayer to God as they begin their journeys.

Although some pilgrimages can take months to walk, I recommend starting with a short half-day or one-day pilgrimage near your home to see if this kind of practice speaks to you. It's important to end your pilgrimage at a particular monument or church, a place where you can take some time to process your experience, reflect, and pray.

Labyrinth: During the Crusades of the Middle Ages, it became too dangerous for pilgrims to travel to the Holy Land to walk in the footsteps of Jesus. They turned to the ancient practice of walking a labyrinth, using it as a finishing point for a more localized pilgrimage. In Chartres, for example, a stone labyrinth was built into the floor of the new cathedral.

Whereas a maze is mainly constructed with the idea of finding your way to a particular point, a labyrinth is constructed for the process of walking toward a destination you can already see. Then, as you approach the center of the labyrinth, the path turns and leads you back toward the edge. This mirrors our life experiences, where we really hope something will happen or we think we're about to arrive somewhere in particular, but life unexpectedly takes us elsewhere.

I've walked outdoor labyrinths a few times when something was weighing very heavily upon me. Often, I start off walking quickly, before finding a rhythm, catching my breath, slowing down a little, and pausing to look around. Feelings like relief, sadness, anger, or joy arise as I continue my walk. Arriving at the center of the labyrinth, I sometimes leave a symbolic item there, such as a stone or a twig that I break, representing something that I'm ready to let go of before I return along the path. At times I've spent up to twenty minutes in the center, looking down at the dirt, pondering what it is I'm trying to relinquish.

In Chapter 9, "Things at Their Depth," Fr. Richard writes about a statue in Assisi where St. Francis gazes "down into the dirt with awe and wonder, which is quite unusual and almost shocking. The Holy Spirit, who is almost always pictured as descending from above, is pictured here as coming from below—even to the point of being hidden in the dirt!" (page 118).

The symbolism of how we move, what we carry, the meandering path we take, and what we're ready to relinquish all make the labyrinth a beautiful embodied exercise. It teaches us to have fewer expectations, to go with the process, and to look more closely at what's "hidden in the dirt" where we stand.

REFLECTIVE EXERCISES

1. Practice at least one of these embodied exercises in the coming days and weeks: find a retreat center and visit for at least half a day, plan a couple of days or more of a walking pilgrimage, or find a labyrinth that you can walk. Pay particular attention to your body more than your intellect during this exercise.

2. Alternatively, you could create your own labyrinth in an open space, turn one of your favorite walks into a pilgrimage, or rearrange a room to make it suitable for a day retreat. This might include gathering plants and flowers, candles and incense, photographs and books that have significant meaning for you. Turn off all technology and pray that you would remain open hearted to whatever comes up for you during your retreat.

The Divine Feminine

Although Jesus was clearly of the masculine gender, the Christ is beyond gender, and so it should be expected that the Big Tradition would have found feminine ways, consciously or unconsciously, to symbolize the full Divine Incarnation and to give God a more feminine character—as the Bible itself often does. (page 122)

Depending on your cultural and religious upbringing, the person of Mary, the mother of Jesus, will have very different connotations. To some she inspires us to pray, visit shrines, and celebrate feast days like that of Our Lady of Guadalupe. To others she's a faithful biblical figure, but she's *not* God, so it's off-putting to imagine praying to her and, seemingly, worshipping her. Fr. Richard writes that Mary is an archetype, a symbol that "constellates a whole host of meanings that cannot be communicated logically" (page 123). Regardless of our religious background, she can show us something important about humanity's relationship with God. In saying yes to the human incarnation of Christ, she represents "*our* eternal yes to God" (page 128).

As a therapist, I regularly hear about clients' relationships with their parents. Those who have had challenging relationships with their fathers often tell me that they have a hard time relating to the masculine symbols of God as Father. The archetypal Mary, on the other hand, symbolizes a loving God in a way that is more accessible for many who struggle to relate to the masculine symbols of God. *"Humans like, need, and trust our mothers to give us gifts,"* Fr. Richard writes, *"to nurture us, and always to forgive us, which is what we want from God"* (page 125).

Take a few moments to reflect on the feminine symbols you've received from your religion, your culture, and your mother.

• What words would you use to describe your relationship with your mother? (You may find it helpful to look at photos and videos from when you were younger. Or, if you have the opportunity, to talk with her about your relationship.)

• What messages have you picked up from your culture and your upbringing about the significance of Mary?

I grew up with a very strong and loving relationship with my mum. From her I learned that I was lovable and that there was a place for kindness and listening in the world. I learned that it didn't matter what I achieved; I would always be loved for who I was. So when I first read Fr. Richard's chapter titled "The Feminine Incarnation," I realized that I most resonate with the more archetypally feminine characteristics of God, symbolized as loving mother and Holy Wisdom (*Sophia*). I love reading passages on *Sophia* in the book of Proverbs and the stories of Jesus in the Gospels that show his kindness toward the sick and the poor. I now understand that the archetypal feminine face of God is what I resonate with the most; I had just never equated it with the archetypal symbol of Mary.

The feminine incarnation can be a source of inspiration to those of us who struggle to relate to God as Father, to those who have been resisting God for a long time and now want to give their yes, or to all those who wish their lives to be characterized by kindness, cooperation, and inclusion. Fr. Richard reminds us of our deep need for this archetypal energy, writing,

Today on many levels, we are witnessing an immense longing for the mature feminine at every level of our society—from our politics to our economics, in our psyche, our cultures, our patterns of leadership, and our theologies, all of which have become far too warlike, competitive, mechanistic, and noncontemplative. We are terribly imbalanced. (page 128)

REFLECTIVE EXERCISES

1. Notice whether this reflection has been challenging for you to read. If so, before moving on to the next questions, journal what thoughts, emotions, and physical sensations are coming up for you right now.

2. Go to a place where you connect with archetypal feminine symbolism—somewhere in nature, an art gallery or church where you can appreciate a painting or a statue, a place of nurturing like a school or a care home—or spend time with your children or those of family and friends. Ask yourself the following questions:

• In what ways do you experience the giving, nurturing, forgiving face of God?

• In what ways do you feel drawn to give to, nurture, and forgive others?

Our Eternal Yes

Mary is all of us both *receiving and handing on the gift.*
We liked her precisely because she was one of us—
and *not* God! (page 124)

F r. Richard tells us that Mary "became the natural
  archetype and symbol for" the Christ-soaked world
out of which Jesus emerged. "She is invariably offering
us Jesus, God incarnated into vulnerability and naked-
ness. . . . Earth Mother presenting Spiritual Son, the
two first stages of the Incarnation" (pages 123–24).

This is deep symbolism on a cosmic scale. The archetypal Mother Earth willingly accepts the task to
nurture the Christ. Though Mary cannot fully understand the implications of her answer, she agrees to play
her small part in serving God. She gives her yes while

unaware of the full extent and significance of the role she's going to play. We have so much to learn from Mary's attitude and openness to God.

Fr. Richard writes,

> In Mary, humanity has said *our* eternal yes to God.
> A yes that cannot be undone.
> A corporate yes that overrides our many noes.
> (page 128)

To some, especially in cultures that value busyness and productivity, Mary can seem passive and taciturn. But her "eternal yes" allowed God to work through her life as a mother, a caregiver, and a conduit for love. I'm reminded of Blaise Pascal's insightful line that "all of man's problems come from his not knowing how to sit quietly in a room."[1] Mary seems to have had this ability, which contrasts with other New Testament figures— the grasping for power of James and John (Mark 10:37) or the busyness of Martha (Luke 10:40). Mary's healthy boundaries created the conditions for Jesus to grow and for God to work.

Over the years I have met many wonderful people who, from a place of goodness and a desire to love, develop a pattern of rescuing others. They care deeply for anyone who is suffering or in need, but since they have poorly defined boundaries in their interpersonal relationships, they take on too much of the other person's burden.

We can go to great, selfless lengths to provide emotional and financial support to our adult children or vulnerable members of our society. But it's important that we don't inadvertently engage in codependent behavior that detracts from others' sense of independence. Otherwise, our well-intentioned interventions can provide short-term fixes that make us feel good about ourselves but disempower others over the long run. If we persist in this behavior, we might find ourselves becoming exhausted and quietly resentful of the needs of others.

Kahlil Gibran beautifully expresses what is needed when he writes, "Let there be spaces in your togetherness. . . . For the pillars of the temple stand apart, and the oak tree and the cypress grow not in each other's shadow."[2]

Mary's yes and her attitude of "*pure being and not doing*" (page 127) are deep lessons for us. Hers is a profound archetypal energy, one that trusts and lets go of all that we might like to do to have a sense of power, control, and even importance in the world. Her presence facilitates Jesus to grow and the Christ to be revealed. Mary shows us how to hold the tension of caring for others while giving them space to grow. She accepts who she is and the role that God has asked of her, while maintaining her focus on what's most important.

In the many images of Mary, humans see our own feminine soul. We needed to see ourselves in her, and say with her, "God has looked upon me in my lowliness. From now on, all generations will call me blessed" (Luke 1:48). (page 124)

REFLECTIVE EXERCISES

1. Reflect on a time when you have taken on too much of another person's burden and have rescued them. How did it feel for you? How did the relationship develop?

2. Now reflect on a time when someone else became too involved, too helpful in your life, possibly crossing some personal boundaries in what they said or did. What was that experience like for you? How did this affect your attitude toward the other person?

3. What is the yes that is being asked of you at this moment? Where in your life might you receive what God is doing and hand it on to others through your presence, through *'pure being and not doing'*?

Embodiment

Jesus did not say, "This is my spirit, given for you," or even "These are my thoughts." Instead, he very daringly said, "This is my *body,*" which seems like an overly physical and risky way for a spiritual teacher, a God-man, to speak. (page 130)

R eflecting on the Eucharistic Meal, Fr. Richard tells us that "in offering his body, *Jesus is precisely giving us his full bodily humanity more than his spiritualized divinity*! 'Eat me,' he shockingly says" (page 130).

This is almost the opposite of what was seen as normative at the time. Fr. Richard writes, "Much of ancient religion portrayed God eating or sacrificing humans or animals, which were offered on the altars, but Jesus turned religion and history on their heads, inviting us to imagine that God would give *himself as food for us!*" (pages 130–31). Even more, he asks us to remember him through a ritual that focuses on his body and our basic physical need to eat.

Despite all this talk and imagery of physicality, many Christians struggle to connect our bodies with our religious experiences. The spiritual life too often involves us staying in our heads and being more concerned with thoughts and ideas than with honoring our emotions, sensations, and embodied experiences.

For several millennia, Western culture and society have relegated the body to the place of least significance, viewing it as something bad or sinful or, at the very least, less important than the mind and soul. René Descartes's famous line *"Cogito, ergo sum"* ("I think, therefore I am")[1] solidified the belief that our self-awareness and ability to think are the proof and pinnacle of our lives as human beings. In the world of religion, this led us away from an incarnational experience of God toward a focus on ideas and truths.

This is why, in discussing the Eucharist, Fr. Richard writes, "The bread and wine, and all of creation, seem to believe who and what they are much more readily than humans do" (page 132). We need to embrace an embodied faith that includes both good theology and a holistic spirituality.

How we treat our bodies can tell us a lot about our view of the world. I have a long history of sports injuries. Every few months I would pull a different muscle in my leg or strain my back and shoulder. But rather than listen to my body and let it heal, I usually listened to voices around me who told me to "push through," to "play on," and that I could "recover later." I pushed through so much, compounding injury after injury, that I reached the point where I wasn't able to run. Eventually, I slowly started to listen to my body, to accept that it's as integral a part of me as my "heart, mind, and whatever we mean by 'soul'" (page 131).

A few years ago, I attended a residential training course where we spent quite a few hours meditating each day. The greatest lesson from the week was how much my colleagues and I learned to deeply listen to our bodies. I experienced pain in places I had never noticed it before and was able to make minor changes in how I sat to help with this. I also learned that I wasn't as hungry as I had previously thought. I had just developed certain eating habits, and when I ate a little less, I had more energy and strength. Although I didn't make massive changes all at once, I did become a lot more aware of how I felt and how I cared for my body.

There is a reason so many people in the Western world have taken up yoga, Pilates, and other gentle body movement exercises in recent decades. We want, I believe, to connect or reconnect with our embodied physicality. We desire to come home and inhabit our embodied selves.

REFLECTIVE EXERCISES

1. Take some time to engage in an embodied activity that you usually enjoy. This can be walking, dancing, swimming, a contemplative sit, a body scan meditation, or anything else that will allow you to more fully connect with your physical body.

2. It's important that you don't strive, push, or compete during this exercise. Let words like *kindness, gentleness,* and *peacefulness* guide you in your selection and approach to the activity.

3. Continue in this embodied exercise until you experience a sense of appreciation for the life that inhabits your body.

Note: If you're in any way doubtful about wanting to complete an embodied exercise, please return to Reflection 16 and reread the section entitled "Staying within Your Comfort Zone While Reflecting on Personal Suffering" before you begin.

Embodied Suffering

We must move our knowing to the bodily, cellular, participative, and thus unitive level. We must keep eating and drinking the Mystery, until one day it dawns on us, in an undefended moment, "My God, I really am what I eat! I also am the Body of Christ." (page 136)

A s a teenager, I struggled with the idea of receiving the Eucharist during our school Masses. "The Body of Christ," the priest would say. "Amen," I had to respond in order to receive the bread. But I didn't believe in the physical Presence of Christ, and it bothered me that I had to make this declaration. My chaplain explained to me, just as Fr. Richard writes, that this communion meal means "communion with God and with God's people, and often with myself" (page 129). It was a breakthrough to realize that my "Amen" is to the fact that we are *all* the Body of Christ, not just the bread.

Fr. Richard writes, "The Eucharistic bread and wine are not a prize for the perfect or a reward for good behavior. Rather they are food for the human journey and medicine for the sick. We come forward not because we are worthy but because we are all wounded and somehow 'unworthy'" (pages 134–35). But this feeling of woundedness can be so intense at times, so all-encompassing, that we struggle to believe that *we* are the Body of Christ. This is particularly the case when we have suffered in our own bodies.

For a long time I looked at the lives that others led—their confidence, their seeming strength—and I imagined that I was entirely alone in my experiences of emotional suffering. I felt so unhappy with myself at one point that I couldn't even glance at my reflection in the mirror. I had embodied some of the damaging narratives of our culture, whose messages made me feel like I was always lacking in some way.

"You have to be strong." "You have to be beautiful." "You have to be thin." We know the damage these kinds of narratives cause, increasingly among men as well as among women. It encompasses eating disorders, compulsive exercising, overeating, sex addictions, and substance abuse. The most fundamental, overarching message is that nobody will love you unless you do certain things with your body, look a particular way, or change your body from what it is.

This emphasis on the outer appearance of our bodies often comes with gender-specific, ethnically relevant messaging that we experience from our earliest years. These narratives, consistent with so much of traditional theological narratives, usually separate our bodies from our hearts, minds, and souls. Under these pressures, it's so easy to lose respect for our bodies and the bodies of others. And none of this even begins to address the deep pain and suffering we feel in our bodies if we've experienced any form of physical or sexual abuse.

We can spend so much time wishing our bodies were different, working to change them, giving up on them, and growing to hate them that we almost welcome a disembodied religion that's focused only on ideas and beliefs. But Jesus met us right at that place, saying this is "my body 'given for you,' 'broken for you,' and my blood 'poured out for you'" (page 135). He, too, was broken. He knew that we, also, would be broken. He knew that we continue to suffer. Christ stands in solidarity with us in a universe that "*is the Body of God, both in its essence and in its suffering*" (page 134).

"In the act of drinking the blood of Christ at this

Holy Meal," Fr. Richard reminds us, "you are consciously uniting yourself with all unjust suffering in the world, from the beginning of time till its end. Wherever there was and is suffering, there is the sympathy and the empathy of God" (page 134).

REFLECTIVE EXERCISES

As with the Reflective Exercises in Reflection 16, it is important that you do not push yourself beyond your comfort zone. If this reflection has been difficult for you to read because of your life experiences, I recommend that you first reread the section entitled "Staying within Your Comfort Zone While Reflecting on Personal Suffering" in Reflection 16. If any aspect of the following exercises seems too much or is unhelpful for you, please feel free to move on.

MIRROR EXERCISE

1. Looking at yourself in the mirror and taking your time to speak slowly and out loud, tell yourself at least ten things you love about who you are. Make sure they are about who you *are* and the process of who you're becoming and not about things you *do* or outcomes you achieve (for example, "I love you because you are kind, because you want to listen to others . . ." rather than "I love you because you are good at your job, because you cook delicious meals . . .").

• Notice how easy or difficult this experience is for you.

• Pay attention to any physical sensations you feel in your body.

2. This can be an emotional experience, so please pray, journal, or reach out to a trusted friend or a mental health professional if you find this embodied exercise to be too challenging.

Atonement

It's time for Christianity to rediscover the deeper biblical theme of *restorative justice,* which focuses on rehabilitation and reconciliation, not punishment. (page 142)

I n the opening pages of his chapter "Why Did Jesus Die?," Fr. Richard explains, "Substitutionary atonement is the theory that Christ, by his own sacrificial choice, was punished in the place of us sinners, thus satisfying the 'demands of justice' so that God could forgive our sins" (page 140). This theory was developed within the norms and values of the eleventh century, when a "medieval code of feudal honor and shame" (page 143) existed across much of Europe.

In those years, Anselm of Canterbury wrote a paper

stating that as a result of humanity's sinful disobedience in the Garden of Eden, "A price did need to be paid to restore God's honor" (page 143). This idea was predicated on a theology where, following St. Augustine's lead, the focus was on the fall of Genesis 3 rather than our primal goodness of Genesis 1. Over the last millennium, this emphasis on the fallen nature of humanity and the need for God's honor to be restored became the most widely accepted theory for why Jesus died.

I remember the day when I first realized the differing emphases on atonement theory among Christians. I was in college when a friend started explaining the Gospel to me. He drew a diagram pointing out the logic of the penal substitutionary atonement theory. I remember his shock when I said, "That's so interesting. It's like the mechanics of why Jesus died. I've never heard that before." He asked me on what basis I called myself a Christian. I started talking about meaning, purpose, the notion that everything is spiritual, my love of Jesus's teachings, and having a sense of connection with God. From the look on his face, I could tell he was concerned for my soul!

But I *did* listen to him. I started taking on this mechanistic approach to understanding what Good Friday was all about. It made my faith simpler, cleaner, and easier to explain to others. But it also shifted my focus from an expansive, soulful life to something that was more reductionistic, guilt ridden, and even fear based.

Over time, my worldview moved to one that was more transactional. Who's in and who's out? What do you believe and what don't you believe? My transformational experiences of spirituality were replaced by a transactional theology *about* God. I had more answers and—dare I say it?—a little less love. As Fr. Richard says, "Try loving your spouse or children that way, and see where it gets you" (page 144).

Attending some church services today, I'm struck by the repetition of these transactional theories for Jesus's death on the cross. These ideas often feature in songs and hymns, in lines like "for God, the just, is satisfied to look on him and pardon me." They are the red thread in many people's interpretation of Scripture, from the Hebrew Scriptures through the New Testament. Sometimes it feels like we're celebrating Good Friday over and over again, every single Sunday; we keep on reminding ourselves of the mechanics of salvation. There tends to be a lot less emphasis on the rest of Jesus's life, his teachings, and the significance of his resurrection.

Fr. Richard writes,

> The Franciscans, however, led by John Duns Scotus . . . claimed that the cross was a *freely chosen revelation of Total Love* on God's part. . . . The cross, instead of being a transaction, was seen as a dramatic demonstration of God's outpouring

love, meant to utterly shock the heart and turn it back toward trust and love of the Creator. (pages 143–44)

In a world that desperately needs transformation and genuine spiritual connection among differing communities, we remain young and immature if we merely focus on how to get in. "In my experience, this way of thinking loses its power as people and cultures grow up and seek actual changes in their minds and hearts," Fr. Richard writes. "Then, *transformational* thinking tends to supplant *transactional* thinking" (page 141).

What difference would it make to the trajectory of our lives, the quality of our relationships, and our respect for those who are different from us if we truly grasped the meaning of these words:

It is not God who is violent. We are.
It is not that God demands suffering of humans. We do.
God does not need or want suffering—neither in Jesus nor in us. (page 146)

REFLECTIVE EXERCISES

1. What were some of your earliest beliefs about why Jesus died on the cross? Do these still ring true for you today?

2. Take a moment to reflect on the view "that the cross was a *freely chosen revelation of Total Love* on God's part" (page 143). If this was true, in what ways would it affect your view of God and your day-to-day experiences of God?

3. Reflect on a relationship in which you have been loving another person in a transactional way. What one practical change could you make to more deeply express your transformational love for them? This action or conversation will communicate that you will continue to love them whether or not they change.

Restoration

[Jesus] did not come to change God's mind about us. It did not need changing. Jesus came to change our minds about God—and about ourselves—and about where goodness and evil really lie. (page 151)

F r. Richard writes that "most of us are still pro-grammed to read the Scriptures according to the common laws of jurisprudence" (page 146). This can leave us too easily satisfied with "an eye for an eye" thinking in how we interpret Scripture and how we view our daily interactions. "I'll babysit for you because I know you'll return the favor." "I expected an invitation to the event; I always invite you." "You owe me for . . ." This way of thinking comes from a quid pro quo perspective on life. It can become our default way of thinking if we view God primarily as a judge who rules by the principles of "an eye for an eye." Fr. Richard writes that juridical thinking "has its important place in human society, but it cannot be transferred to the divine mind. It cannot guide us inside the realm of infinite love or infinite anything" (page 146).

I used to go out of my way to include one group of friends in social activities and to check in and see how they were doing. But I wasn't included in their plans as much, and they didn't check in with me as often. I used this same thinking: "I invited you on the trip; you should have invited me to the party." I couldn't understand it. I felt like this was unfair. Eventually it dawned on me that I was carrying a sense of entitlement: I believed these friends owed me something. I realized they could choose to do whatever they wanted and I could make my own plans—still including them if I wished. This made me feel a lot more relaxed. Without this pressure on our friendships, I ended up becoming closer to some and naturally drifting from others. Moving beyond quid pro quo thinking was a great relief to my social life.

It can take time to move from a juridical mindset toward one that is based on "grace and freedom" (page 153). To get there, we need to begin to see God and all of reality in a very different way. Fr. Richard paraphrases Thérèse of Lisieux, writing that "*there is a science about which God knows nothing—addition and subtraction*" (page 147).

Fr. Richard talks about the human tendency to scapegoat, as described by the philosopher René Girard. This tendency is derived from Israel's Day of Atonement, when the people's sins were symbolically laid on a goat. Fr. Richard writes that "instead of owning our sins, this ritual allowed us to export them elsewhere" (page 149). He continues,

> The image of the scapegoat powerfully mirrors and reveals the universal, but largely unconscious, human need to transfer our guilt onto something (or someone) else by singling that other out for unmerited negative treatment. This pattern is seen in many facets of our society and our private, inner lives. (page 149)

When we project our sins elsewhere, we are unconsciously engaging with our shadow. As we deny our own sins, we dislike those same traits in others and, as Fr. Richard writes, we "hate our own faults in other people" (page 151). But in moving from a punitive view of God to one that is more restorative, we gain the confidence to acknowledge our sins, knowing that healing and acceptance are possible.

A few years ago, I was present at a ritual where the participants acknowledged, as a community, things most of us refuse to acknowledge within ourselves. Fr. Richard brought me to the annual Green Corn Dance at one of the Pueblo villages in New Mexico. The beating drums brought an awed silence as the men and boys emerged from within the sacred *kiva,* a circular stone chamber used for social and spiritual ceremonies. As they processed into the plaza, bare chested, donning moccasins and trailing fox skins behind their waists, they were joined by the women and girls of their clan. The women were barefoot, with turquoise thunderclouds in their hair and rattles and evergreen sprigs in their hands. Thousands of us looked on as the clan walked, danced, sang, and drummed in a procession around the plaza.

Then another group of men appeared, covered in black and white body paint, wearing only loincloths. They each wore a necklace composed of a collection of colored metal penises. The singing and drumming went quiet as these men danced against the oncoming procession, among husbands and wives and in between families, separating them with their meandering movements. "That's the symbol for this year's major sin," whispered Fr. Richard. "Something sexual is separating them from each other." I have never witnessed a more striking ritual. The members of the Pueblo were bold enough, as a community, to publicly shine a light on what usually remains unspoken, private, and denied.

When we have the courage to name our sins, we no longer need to project them onto others. In taking responsibility, we can move from shame-based denial toward something that can be healed and restored within ourselves.

REFLECTIVE EXERCISES

1. Do you tend to see the world more from the quid pro quo, retributive perspective of punishing, weighing, and counting or the grace-filled perspective of healing and restoration?

2. In what ways do you scapegoat others or unknowingly demand their suffering and punishment *before* acknowledging your own faults?

Reflection 28

Cruciform

Jesus agreed to carry the mystery of universal suffering. He allowed it to change him ("Resurrection") and—it is to be hoped—us, so that we
would be freed from the endless cycle of projecting our pain elsewhere or remaining trapped inside
of it. This is the fully resurrected life, the only way
to be, happy, free, loving, and therefore "saved."
(page 147)

W hy is it that we so easily project our pain elsewhere? Another way of asking this is: Why
do we find it so difficult to accept our own pain? For
many of us, it's related to the dominant story line of our
culture, the metanarrative of success. When progress,
results, and comfort form the basis of our highest aspi-

rations, it can be extremely difficult to accept pain and brokenness within ourselves.

From a young age, many of us receive messages like "I need to be good at school," "I need to be popular," "I need to be beautiful," "I need to make money." There's little space for loss and failure in this paradigm, so when we're faced with the inevitable disappointments of life, we tend to hide our pain from others—and even from ourselves. Some of us internalize our pain, leading to physical illness, depression, and low self-esteem. Others project our pain externally, toward individuals and groups we dislike. We usually do a bit of both. But unless we become aware of this unrecognized pain, we will continue to feel inwardly broken and we will project and scapegoat our brokenness onto others.

Eventually, life catches up with us and we are forced to reevaluate our priorities. We need a different story, one whose overarching narrative is far deeper than progress, results, and success. Fr. Richard writes,

> The Divine Mind transforms all human suffering by identifying completely with the human predicament and standing in full solidarity with it from beginning to end. This is the real meaning of the crucifixion. (page 147)

A few months ago, I got to coach someone whose job is to work on the storyboard narrative of animated

EVERY THING IS SACRED

movies. A professional storyteller, she was struggling to see the overarching narrative of her own life. When I asked if she was familiar with the Hero's Journey, she lit up. "Of course. I use it all the time. All our story lines follow this pattern."

In this pattern, the hero, an ordinary person, is invited on an adventure, away from their normal life, to discover a special, unknown world. They hear a call to adventure and receive a mentor and initial help as they descend further into the unknown world to face challenges, tests, and trials. Eventually, they experience an ordeal or a terrible trial, sometimes even dying as a result. But they conquer death and receive a gift to bring back to others within the or-dinary world. When the hero returns, others hardly recognize them at first, as they have been so shaped by this experience of death and rebirth, of descent and resurrection.

It's a common story line we see in movies and books, one that speaks of the transformative importance of facing pain and suffering within ourselves and in the world around us. Fr. Richard writes about how this pattern of the Hero's Journey is similar to "the cross, death, and resurrection narrative of Christianity" (page 247). It is the pattern of spiritual transformation of order, disorder, and reorder that we all go through mul-tiple times throughout our life (pages 244–46). But it is a pattern that is so challenging for us to embrace. We usually don't recognize it until we look back on what we've been through.

I asked the lady who works on the storyboard narrative to think about her own life, to reflect where this pattern is visible. After a little bit of time, the tears began to flow as she started to see her current pain and suffering as being part of a much bigger narrative. She reflected on times she'd suffered before. She'd gotten through tough times in the most unexpected ways, each time learning a new perspective on life. Now here she was again, struggling to understand the challenges and difficulties she was facing in her personal life. By remembering the larger story of the Hero's Journey, she could recognize both the pain of her current situation and the longed-for hope of eventual transformation. She was able to sit with the tension of not being in control, not yet knowing the path ahead, yet trusting that something transformative would come from her current challenges.

Fr. Richard writes that experiences like these are part of "the 'pattern that connects' and solidifies our relationship with everything around us" (page 247). Within this context,

> The cross is not just a singular event. It's a statement from God that *reality has a cruciform pattern*. . . .
>
> Jesus demonstrated that Reality is not meaningless

and absurd, even if it isn't always perfectly logical or consistent. . . .

The Gospel is simply the wisdom of those who agree to carry their part of the infinite suffering of God. (pages 147–48)

The woman's story reminded me of how often I overlook this pattern in my own life. I can see it easily enough in other people, but I'm so caught up in my own struggles at the time that I find it hard to recognize the "pattern that connects" my suffering to all suffering, my transformation and growth to that of everything around me. Fr. Richard tells us,

The people who hold the contradictions and resolve them in themselves are the saviors of the world. They are the only real agents of transformation, reconciliation, and newness. (page 148)

REFLECTIVE EXERCISES

1. In what ways have you bought into the story line of a culture whose highest aspirations are progress, success, and comfort? How has this affected your ability to face personal suffering?

2. Reflecting on your current life challenges in the context of the Hero's Journey, what do you think your call to adventure might be?

Total Love

The cross, then, is a very dramatic image of what it takes to be *usable* for God. It does not mean you are going to heaven and others are not; rather, it means you have entered into heaven much earlier and thus can see things in a transcendent, whole, and healing way now. To maintain this mind and heart over the long haul is true spirituality. (page 153)

The idea that the cross helps us enter into heaven now is strikingly different from how Christianity is often portrayed. Critics accuse Christians of living for the next world rather than actively engaging in this life. And they have a point; we don't carry much good news if our faith is just an escape plan for somewhere else. Fr. Richard writes,

*Christians are meant to be the visible compassion
of God on earth more than "those who are going to
heaven." (page 148)*

One person who embodied this visible compassion
was John Hume, the Nobel Peace Prize laureate and
architect of the Peace Process in Northern Ireland.
While training for the priesthood, he decided to leave
the seminary, get married, and become a teacher. But
seeing the violence taking place in his city of Derry and
inspired by the work of Dr. Martin Luther King Jr., he
became a civil rights activist and politician. For decades,
he insisted that his community move beyond divisive
politics and vengeful reactions to injustice. Rather than
scapegoat another community or become caught up in
a cycle of blame and revenge, he moved toward a win-
win situation that sought to include everybody—
perpetrators and victims across the divide—in a process
of dialogue.

Through peaceful protest and solidarity with all
who suffered, an entire country eventually managed to
break a cycle of systemic retribution. Yet all this came at
great personal cost; not only did Hume's health suffer
from years of tireless work for peace, but his own mod-
erate political party was sidelined after two other dia-
metrically opposed political parties formed a coalition
government together. Yet, in full knowledge that his

own party would likely diminish in influence, he continued in his work toward a lasting peace.

Hume embodied what Fr. Richard calls a "cruciform pattern" (page 147) in the pursuit of restoration and healing—someone who was willing to let go of his personal success for the sake of something far greater. Fr. Richard writes that this " 'way of the cross' . . . never becomes the dominant consciousness anywhere" (page 153). It's counter to any culture that emphasizes only progress or winning at the expense of others. Yet it moves us from transactional tit-for-tat thinking to an inclusive, deeply transformative way of being in the world. Instead of any price needing to be paid, we see "that the cross was a *freely chosen revelation of Total Love* on God's part" (page 143).

Practically speaking, how do we come to see the cross as something restorative and healing? Reassessing our theology, our attitudes, and our outlook on the world is a start. But for lasting change to occur, we need to move beyond "our many modes of scapegoating and self-justification" (page 152). "What, then, does it mean to follow Jesus?" writes Fr. Richard. We must "gain compassion toward ourselves and all others who suffer," which "largely happens on the psychic and unconscious level . . . where all of our hurts and our will to violence lie" (page 152). This self-compassion, in turn, enables us "to embrace the imperfection and even the injustices of our world, allowing these situations to change [us] from the inside out, which is the only way things are changed anyway" (page 148). Below, Fr. Richard suggests an exercise that can begin this process within us.

I believe that we are invited to gaze upon the image of the crucified Jesus to soften our hearts toward all suffering, to help us see how we ourselves have been "bitten" by hatred and violence, and to know that God's heart has always been softened toward us. (page 152)

REFLECTIVE EXERCISE

The following exercise draws on Fr. Richard's "A Dialogue with the Crucified God" (pages 155–58). Fr. Richard suggests, "Wait until you have an open, quiet, and solitary slot of time, then pray it out loud so your ears can hear your own words from your own mouth. In addition, I suggest that you place yourself before a tender image of the crucified Jesus that will allow you to both give and receive" (page 155).

When you reach the second section, "You Speak Back to the Crucified One," write a journal entry or speak your response out loud. This might include expressions of appreciation, understanding, empathy, gratitude, or something else entirely. Don't edit yourself in any way; write or speak as if nobody else will ever hear you, apart from Christ. (Fr. Richard writes his own response, which you may also want to read aloud, on pages 155–58.)

A Dialogue with the Crucified God
Jesus Speaks to You from the Cross

I am what you are most afraid of: your deepest, most wounded, and naked self. I am what you do to what you could love.

I am your deepest goodness and your deepest beauty, which you deny and disfigure. Your only badness consists in what you do to goodness— your own and anybody else's.

You run away from, and you even attack, the only thing that will really transform you. But there is nothing to hate or to attack. If you try, you will become a mirror image of the same.

Embrace it all in me. I am yourself. I am all of creation. I am everybody and every thing.

You Speak Back to the Crucified One

One Suffering

I do believe that the only way out of deep sadness is to go with it *and* through it. . . . *Almost all people are carrying a great and secret hurt, even when they don't know it.* (pages 161–62)

In his book *Adam's Return,* Fr. Richard writes that "all great spirituality is about what we do with our pain."[1] He talks about how "sacred wounding" is central to our maturation and that, like Jacob, we must learn to walk with our limp (Genesis 32:22–32). Rejection from a parent, the untimely loss of a loved one, the abuse of our trust, or a relationship characterized by betrayal are all experiences that can leave us with a deep wound.

Learning to recognize and consciously carry our hurt and sadness is just the beginning. As we "go *with it* and *through it,*" these hurts can become "sacred wounds" that profoundly shape us. This happens when we allow our wounds to bring us on a path of inner healing and self-acceptance. We can offer the transformation of our suffering as a gift to others. But this is a tough path, one that runs contrary to the instincts of an individualistic culture. Fr. Richard writes:

> I wonder if the only way to spiritually hold suffering—and not let it destroy us—is to recognize that we cannot do it alone. When I try to heroically do it alone, I slip into distractions, denials, and pretending—and *I do not learn suffering's softening lessons.* But when I can find a shared meaning for something, especially if it allows me to love God and others in the same action, God can get me through it. I begin to trust the ambiguous process of life. (page 161)

Not long ago, I experienced the pain of losing a friend and mentor. I sobbed at home and grieved alone and barely wanted to go to the wake. But I remember the welcome I received from his family when I went—how we sat around his open casket and ate and drank, told stories, showed photographs, and laughed at our friend Danny's unique ways. Then we cried and held one another as the emotions overcame us. I felt cleansed and whole, having shared my pain and grief with so many others.

Even at work, there can be a time to embrace the suffering we experience and to acknowledge how this affects us and others. I've been present to some beautiful moments with senior leaders, gathered around the boardroom, a sense of tension hanging in the air. Then one person finally opens up, sharing the personal reasons behind their unusual behavior of late. We learn of the stress caused by relational breakdown and workplace conflict. Everyone leans in to listen. Colleagues empathize, and the atmosphere softens as honest discussions ensue. A colleague tells of their struggles to deal with the illness of a loved one. They share our common humanity and return the next day, now with deeper bonds, ready to direct the company for the greater good of their people, their customers, their society—even their planet.

This morning on national radio, a listener wrote in to state that she is in "the silent middle": someone who is not on social media and not in the public eye but who is suffering in silence through the shock and fear of the global coronavirus pandemic. Her emotions and her mental state have suffered, she wrote, and she feels on edge a lot of the time. Her simple, courageous act of writing led to an outpouring of response from others, who admitted how difficult they're finding things.

There is no easy way through this suffering, but there is a sense of solidarity, of being in it together.

"When we carry our small suffering in solidarity with the one universal longing of all humanity, it helps keep us from self-pity or self-preoccupation," writes Fr. Richard (pages 161–62). In sharing our burden, we give others the opportunity to care for us. In moving beyond the shame or embarrassment of how we feel, we offer an invitation for others to face their own silent struggles.

REFLECTIVE EXERCISES

1. What personal suffering are you most aware of today?

2. In what one practical way can you open up to allow others to identify with you and share in your suffering (for example, start a conversation, send an email, ask for help)?

3. In what one practical way can you enter into solidarity with others who suffer (for example, speak out publicly, initiate a chat, make a visit, ask for forgiveness, send a needed gift of food, offer shelter, help an animal, clean a local landscape)?

Reflection 31

All in One Lump

Unless we find the *communal meaning and significance* of the suffering of all life and ecosystems on our planet, we will continue to retreat into our individual, small worlds in our quest for personal safety and sanity. (page 166)

Have you been saved?" It's a question many of us have been asked. Perhaps we've even done the asking. Fr. Richard explains that this individual view of salvation is different from "a fully collective notion," which "echoes *the biblical concept of a covenant love that was granted to Israel as a whole*" (pages 163–64).

As the author of *The Cloud of Unknowing* taught, within this collective, communal view of salvation, "God in Christ dealt with sin, death, forgiveness, salvation *'all in one lump'*"[1] (pages 161–62). This language reflects "the more Eastern church understanding *of the resurrection as a universal phenomenon,* and not just the lone Jesus rising from the dead" (page 163). It is, writes Fr. Richard, "Jesus's major metaphor of the 'Reign of God,' a fully collective notion, which some scholars say is just about all that he talks about" (page 163). But ever since the Great Schism (1054 CE), much of the Western church has missed this universal emphasis.

How do we react to this idea of being lumped in with the collective? This will depend on our personalities, our life experiences, and, most especially, the broader values of our culture. One of the foremost experts in cultural values, Professor Geert Hofstede, defined individualistic societies as places where people have "a preference for a loosely-knit social framework in which individuals are expected to take care of only themselves and their immediate families."[2] Collectivistic societies, on the other hand, are places where people have "a preference for a tightly-knit framework in society in which individuals can expect their relatives or members of a particular ingroup to look after them in exchange for unquestioning loyalty."[3] Of course, individualism and collectivism are part of a continuum, not a binary construct. But even reading those simple definitions, you can notice which one most describes the society within which you grew up and now live.

If we have been brought up in an individualistic

culture, we might find this "fully collective notion," this "one lump" of the "Reign of God," to be shocking, alien, or even dangerous. Communal, collective salvation can jar against some of our most deeply held values. "It is my right." "I am entitled to my own opinion." "I don't agree. I'm going a different way." All these phrases speak of an underlying sense of self as being at least as important, if not more important, than the collective. But Fr. Richard writes,

> Until we start reading the Jesus story through the collective notion that the Christ offers us, I honestly think we miss much of the core message, and read it all in terms of individual salvation, and individual reward and punishment. Society will remain untouched. (pages 163–64)

I have always found this collective notion quite personally challenging. My work as a coach and therapist is all done within the milieu of individualism. I encourage clients to find their voices, to set healthy boundaries with others, to inhabit their bodies, and to live with a degree of personal agency. These are things I believe to be foundationally important. But if we stay focused on our individual happiness and do not grow toward others within the collective, we miss out on the broader message of the Gospel and a deeper experience of life.

In order for us to experience this collective notion,

some movement toward solidarity with others in society is required. We must move beyond empathy to actively taking our place *with* others, experiencing similar conditions to what they are facing. What this looks like will depend on who we are, where we are, and what we feel led to do next.

For some of us, expressing solidarity with others will involve giving our spare bedroom to a refugee family. For others, it might mean volunteering their expertise—accounting, cooking, caring, organizing— to those who are oppressed. Befriending and writing personal letters to the persecuted, getting to know and care for those who are homeless in our neighborhood, or taking part in justice movements of any kind are all ways of tangibly expressing our solidarity with others. It doesn't have to be a grand gesture. Truly listening to a friend in distress is an equally great starting point in shifting our perspective from "me" to the collective "we."

Once I know that all suffering is both *our suffering and God's suffering,* I can better endure and trust the desolations and disappointments that come my way. I can live with fewer comforts and conveniences when I see my part in global warming. I can speak with a soft and trusting voice in the public domain if doing so will help lessen human hatred and mistrust. I can stop circling the wagons around my own group, if doing so will help us recognize our common humanity. (pages 167–68)

REFLECTIVE EXERCISES

1. Reread the definitions of individualistic and collectivistic societies. Which aspects of each societal culture most shaped you during your formative years?

2. Which of these values and perspectives have most influenced who you've become, the daily choices you make in your life, and how you view faith and spirituality today?

3. What is the next simple step toward solidarity with others that you feel led to take? Review what you did after the last reflection, and pray or journal to see what else comes up for you now.

Reflection 32

Resurrection

*"Resurrection" is another word for change, but particu-
larly positive change—which we tend to see only in the
long run. In the short run, it often just looks like death.*
(pages 170-71)

F r. Richard tells us that "the reason we can trust Jesus's resurrection is that *we can already see resurrection
happening everywhere else*" (page 170). From the birth and
death of stars to the way matter changes form, modern
science has shown rebirth to be a "cosmic pattern" con-
stantly working throughout the universe (page 170).
Fr. Richard writes,

*Resurrection is just incarnation taken to its logical
conclusion.*

*If God inhabits matter, then we can naturally believe in
the "resurrection" of the body.*
Most simply said, *nothing truly good can die!* (page
170)

During my early days of faith, I found myself in-
tensely seeking answers to big questions like "What
happens when we die?" and "How do I understand science while resonating with the creation poem in Genesis?" As I encountered more and more of what I could
not possibly know or comprehend, I regularly returned
to the thought that *if* God exists, then *this* is possible too
(even if I don't understand it).

I love how Fr. Richard puts it: "Just as the first creation of something out of nothing (*creatio ex nihilo*)
seems impossible to the human mind, so any notion of
life after death seems to demand the same huge leap of
faith" (page 173). We can have beautiful and coherent
theological beliefs, but what matters most is how we
respond in the moment to the daily deaths that all of us
experience. Do we see abundance, new life, and resurrection, or do we see scarcity and death? "The Preface
to the Catholic funeral liturgy says, 'Life is not ended, it
is merely changed,'" Fr. Richard writes (page 171). The
same holds true for the little deaths we experience in
life.

I once lost my job during an economic downturn.
Over the following weeks, I seesawed between what

Fr. Richard calls "a worldview of scarcity" and a belief in "divine abundance" (page 173). I was scared, worried, and confused. Then I got another job offer. It was a clear step up, a promotion with another employer, but the process of sitting with the uncertainty, with the scarcity, had evoked an even deeper response within. I reflected on the times in my previous job when I had longed to contribute and express myself in other ways. I pictured myself looking back from the distant future and wondered what the older me would say I should do. I decided to take the risk: I turned down the new job and started a completely new venture.

Without doubt, facing the insecurity and uncertainty of this new venture was among the most intense faith journeys of my life. During the first two years, I often shook physically with fear. There was no escaping myself or my understanding and experience of God. Every day I had the opportunity to "positively connect . . . with the Divine Personality" or to "negatively connect, to hate, fear, or oppose" it (page 175). My daily contemplative sits took on a new, profound significance: I would gather up all my concerns (*What if that client doesn't sign? What about cash flow next month?*), allow myself to feel those fears, and then present them as open-ended prayers to God. After each sit, I'd stand up and imagine leaving that day's worries on the seat. I'd bow to them in gratitude for the awareness they brought me of my fearful ego, and then I'd engage with the rest of my day. Slowly, as I focused less on the future and concentrated more on my moment-by-moment presence, I began to trust this new sense of abundance, this new life.

Fr. Richard writes that our view of God affects how we view humanity. When it comes to hope and new life, he says, there tend to be two broad interpretations of what resurrection—both now and in the future—is really about. "Jesus's most consistent metaphor and image for this final state of affairs was some version of a wedding feast or banquet." But amid the backdrop of an "inclusive banquet, available to 'good and bad alike' (Matthew 22:10)," guests want "to set a boundary, a price, an entrance requirement of some sort. Many Christians sadly prefer to read these passages from a worldview of scarcity instead of the Gospel of divine abundance, and this constant resistance to Infinite Love is revealed in the biblical text itself" (pages 172–73).

This response of negativity toward the offer of divine abundance is "called 'sin' or even the state of 'hell,' which [in this sense] is not really a geographical place but a very real state of consciousness" (page 175). Fr. Richard writes,

> The ungenerous mind does not like the wedding banquet. It prefers a dualistic courtroom scene as

its metaphor for the end of time, which is why
Matthew's end-times sheep-and-goats parable is
what most people remember, even though they
do not follow its actual message about care for the
poor, and remember only the scary verdict at the
end. (page 173)

So, how do we respond to the daily deaths we experience *and* embrace resurrection *today*? We embrace
uncertainty. We choose to play with our children while
we fret we should spend time on other things; we notice the traits we dislike in others but reflect on what *we*
might be projecting; we stop trying to win arguments
and seek to understand where others are coming from.

"Courage and confidence is our message! Not
threat and fear," writes Fr. Richard (page 176). "The
New Testament only 'sends out' those (*apostolos*) who
can be 'witnesses to resurrection' (Luke 24:48, Acts
1:22, 3:15b, 13:31), that is, witnesses to this immense
inner and outer conversation that is always going on"
(pages 175–76).

REFLECTIVE EXERCISES

1. Reflect for a moment on some of the daily deaths
you experience. Do you tend to see abundance, new
life, and resurrection, or do you see scarcity and death?
2. Spend a few moments reflecting or journaling on

Jesus's parables about the final state of affairs: the wedding banquet (Matthew 22:1–14; Luke 14:15–23) and the court scene (Matthew 25:31–46). Which aspects of each resonate with you?

3. How might the idea of making courage and confidence your message be manifested today in your attitude, your choices, and your responses to others?

Reflection 33

Revealed as Light

People who are properly aligned with Love and Light will always see in good ways that are not obvious to the rest of us. . . . [They] reveal a high level of seeing, both in depth and in breadth, which allows them to include more and more and exclude less and less. (page 178)

At the Resurrection, Fr. Richard tells us, "Jesus was fully revealed as the eternal and deathless Christ in embodied form" (page 176). This revelation manifested in various ways, beginning with Easter Sunday when "the tombs . . . were opened. And many bodies of those who had fallen asleep were raised up" (page 176).

Over the following days and weeks, those whom Jesus encountered saw the culmination of his teaching and his miracles in his resurrected body. They realized that he was more than just the human Jesus, who lived within the parameters of life and death; he was also the eternal Christ. Fr. Richard writes that "his significance for humanity and for us was made *ubiquitous, personal, and attractive* for those willing to meet Reality through him" (page 178). But for Jesus's first followers, the Resurrection wasn't their first glimpse of this change. In the Gospel accounts, there had been precursors to this moment, in which Jesus was "gradually being revealed as 'Light'" (page 177)—most notably in the Transfiguration.

In the same way, we do not have to wait for our death and final resurrection before "Love and Light" is revealed within us. Fr. Richard tells us that "most of us, if we are listening and looking, also have such resurrection moments in the middle of our lives, when 'the veil parts' now and then" (page 177).

This experience of resurrection can come about at any time, but often we notice this "parting of the veil" after a prolonged period of darkness. It might be that we are in the depths of grief, barely able to eat or sleep. But over time, things begin to change. We find ourselves going to restaurants, seeing friends again. We talk about our loss and our pain, but sometimes we laugh as well. The deep pain turns into a low ache, and we slowly begin to function again.

Or maybe we have been carrying a great hurt for a long time. We feel the searing pang of unforgiveness, the anger that returns when we think of that person, until we reach the point when we've carried it long enough. Without holding out for the other person to finally change, we decide to unreservedly forgive them. As Fr. Richard writes,

> When you've been included in the spaciousness of divine love, there is just no room for human punishment, vengeance, rash judgment, or calls for retribution. We certainly see none of this small-mindedness in the Risen Christ after his own rejection, betrayal, and cruel death; we don't see it even from his inner circle, or in the whole New Testament. I really cannot imagine a larger and more spacious way to live. (page 72)

The "parting of the veil" experience that most excites me is when I witness people taking off their personas and truly accepting themselves for the first time. They "peel [their] own image from the mirror" (page 234, excerpt from Derek Walcott's poem "Love after Love"), seeing and loving themselves for who they are rather than for who they have been trying to be.

Fr. Richard tells us that Jesus "had to live his life with the same faith that we must live, and also 'grow in wisdom, age, and grace' (Luke 2:40), just as we do" (page 177). Along the way, we experience these partings of the veil, the unfolding of this resurrection in our own lives. Fr. Richard writes,

> Resurrection is about the whole of creation, it is about history, it is about every human who has ever been conceived, sinned, suffered, and died, every animal that has lived and died a tortured death, every element that has changed from solid, to liquid, to ether, over great expanses of time. It is about you and it is about me. It is about everything. The "Christ journey" is indeed another name for every thing. (page 186)

REFLECTIVE EXERCISES

1. What "resurrection moments" have you experienced in the midst of grief, pain, and challenge?

2. What caused these experiences to move from "death" toward "resurrection" (for example, a thought you had, something you read, a conversation with someone, or an emotional state that led to this change)?

3. In what ways are you currently being invited to align "with Love and Light," to "include more and more and exclude less and less"? Journal your response.

Hell

If you are frightened into God, it is never the true God that you meet. If you are loved into God, you meet a God worthy of both Jesus and Christ. How you get there is where you arrive. (page 181)

Fr. Richard writes, "It is hard to talk about hell calmly or intelligently with most people who have been Christians from childhood" because, in so many cases, they have come to see "God the Father as Punisher in Chief, an angry deity who consigns sinners to eternal torment and torture *instead of as the one who is life itself*" (page 180). The image of hell looms large in our psyches. For some, even reading the title of this reflection might be off-putting, such is the degree of negative connotation that the word carries.

The New Testament says that Jesus descended "'into the lower regions'" and "'went and made a proclamation to the spirits in prison'" (Ephesians 4:9; 1 Peter 3:19, page 180). These images of a descent into hell paint a picture of a place that resembles the Greek Hades, the Hebrew places of Sheol and Gehenna, "or even some notion of Limbo" (page 180). They are a stark contrast to "Dante's version [of hell, which] became the dominant one, forming our Western mind more than any other" (page 181). In his *Divine Comedy,* the poet created an image of "a punishing God" who is "dualistic and frightening" (page 181) in how he systematically deals with sinners in hell.

I remember feeling shocked by the elaborate and brutal punishments of the souls in Dante's hell, such as lying in burning tombs or being whipped by demons. Seeing these scenes depicted in art on the walls of the Sistine Chapel and on the inside of the cupola of the Duomo in Florence further enhanced my sense of fear and disgust. This "fire and brimstone" imagery "about the wrath of God" is etched in my memory (page 181). Fr. Richard says this message continues to be communicated through contemporary song and sermon. "Many of us were taught a vision of God as Tormentor when we were small, impressionable children, and it got deposited in the lowest part of our brain stems, like all traumatic injuries do" (page 180).

The Eastern Orthodox traditions talk about the
" 'Harrowing of Hell,' " in which Jesus sets out to destroy death and pull imprisoned souls "out of hell"
(page 181). But our brain's confirmation bias means
that we are naturally—and usually unconsciously—on
the lookout for what we believe we already know.
Does our vision of hell have more in common with
Dante's medieval imagination than the one in the
New Testament, which emphasizes God's goodness? If
so, this points to our own wider worldview of retributive justice and punishment more than it does the in-
tent of Scripture. God's attitude toward his people in
the books of Habakkuk and Ezekiel is *" 'But I will love
you even more until you come back to me!' "* writes Fr.
Richard (page 184). "God always outdoes the Israel-
ites' sin by loving them even more! This is God's restorative justice . . . [which] *makes things right at their
very core*" (page 184).

Fr. Richard reminds us that "Jesus roundly rejects"
notions of "top-down" "clear winners and clear losers"
(page 182). Instead, Jesus says, " 'Whoever is not against
us is for us' " (Mark 9:40), and that " 'God causes his sun
to rise on bad as well as good, and causes it to rain on
honest and dishonest alike' " (Matthew 5:45) (page
182). Fr. Richard notes that Jesus "makes outsiders and
outliers the heroes of most of his stories" (page 182).

How do you react to this last paragraph? Do you,
like me, immediately focus on theological arguments,

evidence, books you've read, or sermons you've heard on the topic? What about your emotional reactions? Do you feel anger, fear, shame, sadness, or something more akin to surprise, relief, or love as you reflect on these contrasting visions of hell? We might *want* to believe that "God grows more and more *nonviolent* through the Scriptures," that he focuses on "infinite love, mercy, and forgiveness," (page 183) but we struggle to feel like that's possible or right.

To begin to accept an alternative of what is meant by *hell,* we have to be willing to challenge deeply held notions and develop new connotations. And change takes time, particularly when a belief, idea, or hypothesis is so deeply rooted in the recesses of our brain. We need to be reminded, again and again, that

As long as you operate inside any scarcity model, there will never be enough God or grace to go around. Jesus came to undo our notions of scarcity and tip us over into a worldview of absolute abundance—or what he would call the "Reign of God." The Gospel reveals a divine world of infinity, a worldview of enough and more than enough. Our word for this undeserved abundance is "grace": "Give and there will be gifts for you: full measure, pressed down, shaken together, and running over, poured into your lap" (Luke 6:38). (pages 184–85)

REFLECTIVE EXERCISES

1. In what ways do you relate to a retributive image of hell as a place of punishment? Has the understanding of God as a punisher and tormentor affected you in any way?

2. How does this match your understanding and experience of God's restorative justice that brings healing and *"makes things right at their very core"* (page 184)?

3. Given this reflection, and others on resurrection and restoration, what does *hell* mean to you?

Universal Encounter

> Like Mary, we must somehow hear our name pro-
> nounced, must hear ourselves being addressed and
> regarded by Love, before we can recognize this
> Christ in our midst. And like Mary, we usually
> need to start with the concrete encounter before
> we move to the universal experience available to
> all. (page 192)

Mary Magdalene is known as the "'apostle to the apostles,'" the first "'witness to the resurrection' (Acts 1:22)," (page 192) who was charged with telling everyone about Jesus rising from the dead (page 192). She had been "a follower and friend of Jesus after he had cast seven demons out of her" and was "mentioned as many as twelve times throughout the Gospels (more

than most apostles)" (page 190). A "consistent and faithful witness" (page 190) to Jesus, in his life as well as his
death, Mary became the first person to recognize Jesus
on that first Easter Sunday. As Fr. Richard writes, she

> turns around and sees a man whom she doesn't
> recognize. Mary supposes he is the gardener (John
> 20:15) and asks him where he has taken Jesus.
> Then, in one of the most dramatic moments in
> the Gospels, the man simply pronounces her
> name, "Mary!" . . .
> "Turning to face him," she cries out, "Rabbuni!"
> which means "Master" (John 20:13–16). In-
> stantly, Mary sees the one before her in a different
> way, you might say *relationally instead of merely*
> *physically.* She realizes it is still Jesus, but he has
> fully become the Christ. (pages 190–91)

It is quite remarkable how quickly Mary accepts
this phenomenal change that has taken place in her
friend and teacher. Faced with a similar situation, I
wonder how you or I might react. I've always found it
interesting to bump into old friends and acquaintances,
to see how they're doing and notice how they've
changed. Within moments I can usually sense whether
they're open to recognizing how I've changed since our
last encounter, to seeing the person I've become. These
can be unusual encounters, especially if the friend or

acquaintance insists on holding on to an image of who I was.

A few years ago, a childhood friend, who is now a politician, was a guest of honor at my high school's alumni networking event. Although he had attended a different school, he told me, "I didn't expect you to be here." The implication was that based on the images and memories he had of me from our childhood, in his mind it didn't make sense for me to be attending an event like this. On another occasion, I was having dinner with an old college friend when he asked a pointed question: "You're not still into religion, are you?" He seemed shocked by my answer. Apparently I had been coming across as quite "normal" up to that point in our conversation!

In contrast, how beautiful it is to meet people you used to know, friends or acquaintances from what seems like another life entirely, and find that they are interested in who you are today. This usually happens with people who have undergone major change themselves. Experiences from their own lives have led them to re-evaluate their priorities and reassess who they are. You begin talking, and your slightly embarrassed, standoffish demeanor softens as you relax and let down your guard. Each of you *sees* the other person and allows yourself to be seen.

So it is with Mary Magdalene and Christ. Fr. Richard writes that she "came to full spiritual knowing quickly because it was a *knowing through love relationship, and presence itself.* Notice that she knew and trusted Jesus's voice, even when she couldn't recognize him" (page 193). He continues,

> Like Mary, we must somehow hear our name pronounced, must hear ourselves being addressed and regarded by Love, before we can recognize this Christ in our midst. . . .
> I want you to notice that Mary took her journey not by *grasping* on to the old Jesus, but by letting him introduce her to the even larger Christ. (pages 192–94)

When Jesus tells Mary, "'Do not cling to me' (John 20:17a)" (page 191), it doesn't seem to adversely affect her. She has accepted that Jesus made the change to the Christ. She is not holding on to his old self, to their friendship as it was before. She instantly recognizes that things are different, that "Christ is untouchable *in singular form* because he is omnipresent *in all forms*" (page 191).

REFLECTIVE EXERCISES

1. Take a moment to reflect on long-standing relationships in your life where you've experienced a degree of frustration or conflict. Do you recognize who the other

person has become? Does the other person see how you've changed and who you've become?

2. Take some time to journal and pray about these relationships.

3. Have you allowed your understanding of and relationship with God to develop and change from where it started?

Paul's Personal Encounter

The fact that Paul didn't know Jesus in person
makes him the perfect voice to name the Christ
experience for all of us who come after him. . . .
His is a classic description of conversion, and it follows the typical progression *from self-love, to group
love, to universal love.* (pages 195–96)

F or many, the mention of the apostle Paul can pro-
duce a strong reaction. We've heard years of teaching based on the writings of this man who is regarded
by many as legalistic and sexist. But Fr. Richard writes
that there's another way of viewing Paul—as someone
who witnessed Christ's presence despite never having
known Jesus in the flesh and who sought to extend

that witness to people who had previously been excluded from the Christian community:

> Rather than reading Paul's thought primarily as arguments about sin and salvation, as Christians have long tended to do, I want to read Paul as a witness to both personal and cultural transformation, which he himself went through. Jesus represents the personal and Christ the cultural, historical, and social levels. Paul really teaches both. (page 195)

Fr. Richard writes that Paul's three days of blindness after his Damascus road encounter, where "he took no food or water . . . and began his transition to a 'new world' in Christ . . . symbolizes a time of necessary transitioning to a new knowledge" (page 195). From that moment on, Paul moved "away from narrow religion and into a universal vision" (page 195). In many ways, Fr. Richard encourages us to be open to a similar transition in how we view Paul's teachings—particularly when it comes to sin.

Fr. Richard tells us "that sin for Paul was actually a combination of group blindness or corporate illusion, and the powerlessness of the individual to stand against it . . . along with systemic evil" (page 196). "Paul's notion of sin," he writes, "comes amazingly close to our

present understanding of addiction," where we unconsciously engage in unhealthy patterns of behavior, barely
aware that we are enthralled with "'mere rubbish' (Philippians 3:8)" (page 197). Even when we glimpse the
effects of what we're doing, it doesn't always lead to any
change in our behavior. This is so different from viewing sin as a list of particular behaviors that we try our
hardest to stop but end up doing anyway.

Paul's view of salvation, too, is different from what
we usually assume. Fr. Richard writes, "In the undis-
puted seven original letters of Paul, he does not speak of
personal forgiveness as much as of God's blanket forgiveness of all sin and evil. Sin, salvation, and forgiveness are always corporate, social, and historical concepts
for the Jewish prophets and for Paul" (page 198). For
those who have embraced a legalistic understanding of
Paul's writings, this is a huge shift. Each of us can heal,
grow, face our shadows, and deal with habits that we
know are hurting us, but if we don't address the broader
context of our family relationships, our organizational
norms, and our societal values, very little will change
for those around us and those still to come.

Instead of personal purity or individual salvation,
"Paul . . . was convinced that only corporate goodness
could ever stand up to corporate evil—thus his emphasis on community building and 'church'" (pages 196–
97). Church was meant to be "an alternative society,"

writes Fr. Richard, "to show that the Christ people really are different from mass consciousness" (page 200). But with fewer people attending weekly services and raising their families within the traditional structures of faith communities, the manifestation of this corporate body is shifting.

"I do encounter Christians who are living their values almost every day, and more and more are *just doing it* ('orthopraxy'), without all the hype about how right they are ('orthodoxy')," writes Fr. Richard (page 201). "Think tanks, support groups, prayer groups, study groups, projects building houses for the poor, healing circles, or mission organizations" are all examples of the many "para-church organizations . . . that live Christian values in the world" (pages 200–201). These communities can move us beyond the emphasis on individual behavior and model an alternative way of being that we wouldn't have experienced on our own. They give us a sense of hope and help us see that we are part of a much larger story.

"Remember, it is not the brand name that matters," writes Fr. Richard. *"It is that God's heart be made available and active on this earth"* (page 201).

REFLECTIVE EXERCISES

1. Reflect for a moment on some of your behaviors that might constitute individual sin (for example, an addiction, greed, lust, a dismissive attitude, and so on).

• What aspects of your family and your upbringing have shaped these sinful behaviors?

• Are you reacting from a place of hurt, scarcity, or fear?

• Are you usually conscious of these behaviors, or are they part of your shadow, whereby everyone else sees them and even tells you about them but you struggle to understand what they mean?

• Can you see the effects that these behaviors have on others?

Journal what comes up for you and pay attention to the broader systemic context of these behaviors.

2. Reflect on your experience of church or other faith communities. In what ways have you experienced a collective "alternative society" that has stood "up to corporate evil" (pages 197, 200)? In what ways have your religious communities remained "a model whereby people live almost entirely in the world, fully invested in its attitudes toward money, war, power, and gender" (page 200)?

3. What would it mean for you to further move from an emphasis on how right you are (orthodoxy) toward an emphasis on *"just doing it"* (orthopraxy)?

Both . . . And . . .

> If we've been kept from appreciating a cosmic no-
> tion of Christ up to now . . . it's because we have
> tried to understand a largely nondual notion with
> the dualistic mind that dominates Western ratio-
> nalism and scientism. . . . The binary mind, so
> good for rational thinking, finds itself totally out
> of its league in dealing with things like love, death,
> suffering, infinity, God, sexuality, or mystery in
> general. (pages 203, 205)

Engaging with some passages of Scripture and themes within *The Universal Christ* can be chal-lenging to the rational mind. We want clear, unequivo-cal answers that help us categorize where this knowledge or insight fits within our current worldview. Is it this or is it that? Is it in or is it out? Having clear answers to these kinds of dualistic questions helps us feel confident and in control. But when there are multiple layers of meaning to a text, it can leave our rational minds feeling anxious and uncertain.

Fr. Richard writes that dualistic, "inherently argumentative Christianity . . . set us on a very limited 'rational' way of knowing" and that "most of us were not told that we needed to install 'software' different from the either-or, problem-solving, all-or-nothing mind that we use to get us through the day" (pages 204, 203).

One of the side effects of this dualistic way of seeing is that we reduce complex experiences to sets of binary alternatives: "I can either focus on my career or be a family person." Or, "My friend/partner started this fight, so the whole thing is their fault." Fr. Richard writes, "The two alternatives are always exclusionary, usually in an angry way: things are either totally right or totally wrong, with me or against me. . . . The binary mind provides quick security and false comfort, but never wisdom" (page 205).

We need to develop a capacity for "both . . . and . . ." thinking so that we can embrace the complexities inherent in daily life. This involves reframing how we see our experiences while at the same time practicing being honest about what we think and feel: "I'm in love with this person, but I'm angry with them right now." "This child is behaving badly, but they're still fundamentally good." "Neither my friend/partner nor I are totally in the right or totally in the wrong; we've both played a part in this disagreement."

If we don't learn to live in this nondualistic way, we will reduce our experiences, beliefs, and understandings to overly simplistic categories that miss much of the subtlety and complexity of life. We may think we are acting rationally when we're actually seeking to be in control. We try to draw neat lines and boundaries around beautiful, expansive concepts like friendship and faith. Eventually, Fr. Richard writes, we end up with a mindset that has "no room for 'sinners' or outsiders of almost any sort—which was of course the exact opposite of Jesus's message and mission" (page 204).

The key to this nondualistic way of seeing and living is to embrace "a contemplative way of knowing" (page 204). This means that instead of analyzing and categorizing every experience and idea in concrete black-and-white terms, we pay attention to the gray areas, the "both . . . and . . ." possibilities in our lives. We patiently wait *"for the gaps to be filled in"* without insisting *"on quick closure or easy answers"* (page 8). Fr. Richard writes,

> The contemplative mind can see things in their depth and in their wholeness instead of just in

parts. . . . It is not our metaphysics ("what is real") that is changing, but our epistemology—*how we think we know what is real.* (page 205)

REFLECTIVE EXERCISES

1. Are there areas in your life where you tend toward "either . . . or . . ." dualistic thinking (for example, "Either she replies to my email today or I'm not working with her anymore"; "Either I learn to meditate this year or I won't try again")? Journal about your experiences of what's good and what's not so good about these dualisms.

2. Now turn each of those situations into "both . . . and . . ." thoughts (for example, "Whether or not she emails me back, I will seek to maintain an appropriate working relationship with her—I just won't assign her the same tasks as before"; "I'm going to try my best to meditate each day for forty days, after which I can choose to continue or to stop—there's no pressure either way"). Journal about how it feels to see your options from this nondualistic perspective. Does it change how you view or how you feel about these scenarios?

Reflection 38

Contemplative Practice

If we have some good teachers, we will learn to
develop a conscious nondual mind, a choiceful
contemplation, some spiritual practices or disci-
plines that can return us to unitive consciousness
on an ongoing and daily basis. (page 209)

I n an earlier reflection, we explored Fr. Richard's belief that we naturally enter into these unitive, nondual states of consciousness when we experience great
love and great suffering. These experiences, according
to Fr. Richard, are God's *"primary tools for human transformation"* (page 207). But in order for us to develop an
embodied, grounded spirituality, it's important that we
don't rely exclusively on these experiences of love and

suffering; we need to regularly engage in some form of contemplative practice.

Over the last number of decades there has been a resurgence of interest in Eastern spirituality in the West, most especially in Buddhism. Fr. Richard writes that "Buddhism and Christianity shadow each other. They reveal each other's blind spots" (page 210). He says,

> Buddhism is more a philosophy, a worldview, a set of practices to free us for truth and love than it is a formal belief system in any notion of God. . . . (page 211). . . . In telling you mostly *how* to see, Buddhism both appeals to us and threatens us because it demands much more vulnerability and immediate commitment to a practice—more than just "attending" a service, like many Christians do. (page 211)

I was fortunate enough to have been taught to meditate within the Christian tradition from the age of twelve. My schoolteacher guided our religion class in imagination exercises from the Gospels, as well as embodied contemplative sits. He taught us to pay as much attention to our bodies and our breathing as to the Scripture that we read before entering into contemplative silence.

I was surprised to learn that contemplative exercises are considered Eastern, outside influences, or even heretical practices within some Christian traditions. We have only to look to the Desert Mothers and Fathers and centuries of monasticism to see how deeply rooted contemplative practices are within the Christian tradition. But given the "entrepreneurial instinct" of an "extroverted," "dynamic and outflowing" Western Christianity, writes Fr. Richard, "we became a formal and efficient religion that felt that its job was to tell people *what to see instead of how to see*" (pages 210–11). When this becomes our main focus, we naturally place less emphasis on contemplation, and our religious activities "seem to have little effect on *how* the human person actually lives, changes, or grows" (page 212).

We need to develop ways of embracing a fully incarnational Christianity, "not just personal enlightenment, but also social connection and communion— which ironically ends up being divine connection too" (page 212). Cultivating a contemplative practice helps move us beyond "the *what* and *Who* of religion" toward "*how to see*" and how to be (pages 211–12).

REFLECTIVE EXERCISES

1. Read over the following script for a self-guided contemplative sit (or ask someone to read it to you). You will need a countdown timer (a clock or a cell phone timer). Having a prayer bell (a digital or physical bell) to indicate the start and end of the contemplative sit is recommended but not necessary. You can sound the

prayer bell and start the countdown timer once you finish reading the script below, pausing after each phrase. Some people find it helpful to close their eyes during the silence of the sit. The instructions in parentheses are guidelines for you and do not have to be read aloud.[1]

If this is your first time engaging in a contemplative sit, I suggest starting with two to five minutes of silence after reading the script aloud. Over time, with daily practice, this can increase to as many as twenty minutes per day.

As I begin my contemplative sit, I take a few moments to notice my posture. Becoming comfortable in my seat, I sit slightly forward so that my spine is no longer touching the back of the seat. I become aware of both my feet touching the floor, grounding me in the present moment. I focus on my back and my neck, allowing them to find their most aligned and neutral positions.

As I begin my contemplative sit, I remember that I'm not trying to achieve anything. There are no goals. I am simply becoming aware of this moment. Becoming aware of my presence in this moment. Noticing any distractions, thoughts, judgments, decisions, and ideas that cross my mind and paying attention to any emotions that I feel. I choose to let go of all these for now. Instead, I focus on my moment-by-moment experience of being present to what is, God's Presence, the Larger Field, en Cristo.

When I become distracted, frustrated, or confused, I consciously return to offering up my moment-by-moment presence to God's Presence by repeating a sacred word, such as Yahweh or Jesus, or simply by focusing on my breath—in and out—whenever distracting thoughts or emotions come up for me. I know that God's Presence is already within me, whether I'm aware of it or not. No offering up is needed—I am offering in.

Now read the following text of Psalm 46:10 aloud, pausing after each line. The silent portion of your sit will follow.

Be still and know that I am God
Be still and know that I am
Be still and know
Be still
Be

Now start the countdown timer and ring a prayer bell to indicate that the contemplative sit has begun. Ring a prayer bell to indicate that the contemplative sit has finished after two, five, ten, fifteen, or twenty minutes, whichever time frame you have selected.

2. Journal what this experience was like.
3. Repeat this contemplative sit each day, ideally for a minimum of forty days, as practicing anything for this

period of time helps us form a new habit. Engaging in the regular practice of a contemplative sit helps us "to install 'software' different from the either-or, problem-solving, all-or-nothing mind that we use to get us through the day" (page 203) and embrace a more contemplative "both . . . and . . ." perspective on life.

The Contemplative Path

Contemplation allows us to *see* things in their wholeness, and thus with respect. . . . You begin to see there's a correlation between how you do anything and how you do everything else, which makes you take the moment in front of you much more seriously and respectfully. You catch yourself out of the corner of your eye, as it were, and your ego games are exposed and diminished. (pages 215–16)

As we engage in contemplative practices, it is important to remember that the precise manner in which we contemplate is not as important as the lesson that the practice teaches us: to let go of our egos and increasingly see the world with wholeness and respect.

We choose a path of descent, instead of ascent, so we can live in a "holistic and inclusive" way (page 216).

For those who struggle with the silence of a contemplative sit, Fr. Richard mentions several other approaches to practice. There is the "deep wisdom of goalless walking," which "Type A personalities" might appreciate, while others might find "music, dancing, and running" more helpful (page 215). Another approach is what scholar Barbara Holmes refers to as "crisis contemplation," a form of practice that "arose out of necessity during slavery, beginning in the Middle Passage when people were transported across the ocean as human cargo. In times such as this, contemplation becomes the soul's strategy of survival."[1]

Fr. Richard writes,

> Barbara teaches how the Black experience of moaning together, singing spirituals that lead to intense inner awareness, participating in de facto liturgies of lamentation, and engaging in nonviolent resistance produced a qualitatively different—but profound—contemplative mind. (page 214)

Depending on our personalities, our tradition, or our cultural background, we'll find ourselves drawn to different contemplative practices at different times. In the winter I want to wrap up in a warm blanket, with a mug of something hot in hand, and light a candle or incense stick in the half light of morning. I read a short meditative passage from a book or from Scripture before starting a contemplative sit. When I lived in the city, this was my year-round practice, as the busy, noisy streets distracted me from any kind of walking contemplation. But now that I live in a suburb near the coast, my summer practices might include a contemplative walk along the beach or a sit in my garden or at the top of a hill I've just climbed. Even a gentle swim in the cold Irish Sea helps me reset and reengage with life in a fundamentally different way.

Regardless of where we live, in the wilderness or in the bustle of a city, we need to experiment and discover what forms of contemplative practices work best for us. "It is largely a matter of your inner goal and intention, and whatever quiets you in body, mind, and heart," writes Fr. Richard (page 215). Our spiritual practices are exercises in letting go so that we can experience the Universal Christ in all of life. They help us engage in the path of descent, as opposed to a path of self-aggrandizement.

Fr. Richard writes, "Philosophies and religions are either Ascenders, pointing us *upward* (toward the One, the Eternal, and toward Absolutes), or they are Descenders, pointing us *downward* (toward the many, the momentary, and toward the earth), seldom both—and, even less, both at the same time."[2] In *The Universal Christ,* he says that he trusts "the descending form of religion much more" than any form of "'climbing religions'" (page 217). "It is not insignificant that Christians chose the cross or crucifix as their central symbol" (page 216), as it is all about "unlearning, letting go, surrendering, serving others, and *not the language of self-development*" (page 217).

When our dominant culture places its emphases on progress and achievement, contemplative practices are particularly important. They guide us away from a trajectory of climbing, Fr. Richard writes, and ground us in the more transformative path of descent.

> You decide not to push yourself to the front of the line, and something much better happens in the back of the line. You let go of your narcissistic anger, and you find that you start feeling much happier. You surrender your need to control your partner, and finally the relationship blossoms. Yet each time it is a choice—and each time it is a kind of dying. (pages 218–19)

REFLECTIVE EXERCISES

1. Aside from contemplative sits, what other type of contemplative practices would you like to try? What people, books, or kind of practical research will help you start?

2. In what relationship or social situation could you choose "a kind of dying" today?

Reflection 40

Finding Balance

In our Living School here in New Mexico, we teach a methodology that we call our "tricycle." It moves forward on three wheels: *Experience, Scripture, and Tradition,* which must be allowed to regulate and balance one another. Very few Christians were given permission, or training, in riding all three wheels together, much less allowing experience to be the front wheel. (page 213)

In many ways, this book has been an invitation for us to reflect on the ways our faith traditions and our readings of Scripture have influenced our experience of God. Fr. Richard spends a lot of time writing about experience because it's often the most neglected wheel of the "tricycle" he describes above. "Up to now," he writes, "Catholics and Orthodox have used Tradition in both good and bad ways, Protestants used Scripture in both good and bad ways, and neither of us handled experience very well at all" (page 213).

It can be helpful to trace our own journeys by understanding how we have emphasized the "tricycle" of *Experience, Tradition,* and *Scripture* throughout our lives. When some of my friends completed the group guide to *The Universal Christ,* several of them observed that they have heavily relied on only one or two of the tricycle wheels, essentially turning it into a bicycle or even a unicycle.

For me, the *Traditions* of my Catholic upbringing initially struck me as superstitious and off-putting. So I disregarded the teachings and the symbols and focused on my day-to-day life *Experiences.* But as I pursued life *Experiences* that were not anchored in any kind of spirituality, I felt disappointed and disillusioned, which led me to approach *Scripture* in a meaningful way for the first time. I loved it; I learned so much and it resonated with me in an amazing way. But over time I began to lean too heavily upon it. I developed an overly literal reading of texts that produced a reductionistic, dualistic worldview. I ended up returning to study theology and developed a broad and deep awareness of *Tradition* across all Christian denominations, tracing the evolution of key ideas and sacraments. Very, very slowly I began to see the importance of rationally assessing *Scripture* and *Tradition* in a way that honors my daily lived *Experiences.*

The "tricycle" is a wonderful metaphor for how we holistically connect with the depths of our spirituality. Riding all three wheels at the same time is not something we ever completely master. Depending on what's happening in our lives, we will usually emphasize one or two wheels over the other one or two. But simply being aware of the wheels can remind us of the foundational function of religion: to *"re-ligio,"* to reconnect with reality (page 239).

This book of reflections has sought to reconnect us, in a practical way, to knowing that "'there is only Christ. He is everything and he is in everything' (Colossians 3:11)" (page 43). His is a path of descent that displays how "*God loves things by becoming them*" (page 16). It's a path that we can follow as we lovingly engage with God, ourselves, and the world around us.

The practices, symbols, and spiritual exercises we engage in remind us that "'*unless the single grain of wheat falls into the ground, it remains just a single grain. But it if dies, it will bear much fruit*' (John 12:24)" (page 218). As we come to see this more and more, the process "will feel more like unlearning than learning, more like surrendering than accomplishing" (page 222). "Such daily and 'necessary suffering' is the price of both enlightenment for the self and compassion for others" (page 218).

My hope is that these reflections and exercises have encouraged you to see God in the breadth of all things and to experience the Christ in the depths within—or, as Fr. Richard so beautifully writes,

> To experience—and to *know*—that the Christ, you, and every "stranger" are all the same gazing. (page 234)

REFLECTIVE EXERCISES

1. As we come to the last of the Reflective Exercises in this book, take some time to trace your own journey of the "tricycle."

• Which of the three wheels did you first emphasize in your faith life?
• How did this affect your day-to-day living?
• In what ways could revisiting this "tricycle" from time to time encourage you to connect more holistically with your faith and spirituality?

2. Reread the various Reflective Exercises in this book and identify a few that you would like to revisit and possibly even develop in the future. Some of the longer exercises you might wish to return to include the following:

- Reflection 6—spending time in nature
- Reflection 10—making contact with an old friend
- Reflection 20—further self-learning with the Enneagram, MBTI, or any of the tools mentioned on page 115 of *The Universal Christ*
- Reflection 21—a retreat, a pilgrimage, or a labyrinth
- Reflection 24—an embodied exercise of your choice
- Reflection 25—the mirror exercise of self-love
- Reflection 28—further self-learning with research into your path on the Hero's Journey
- Reflection 29—Dialogue with the crucified God
- Reflection 30—solidarity with those who suffer
- Reflection 38—practicing a contemplative sit

Notes

REFLECTION 1

1. According to Mihaly Csikszentmihalyi, we have the capacity to consciously process up to 126 bits of data per second. See Mihaly Csikszentmihalyi, *Flow: The Psychology of Optimal Experience* (New York: HarperCollins, 1990), 29. With far more data than that available to us each second, our brain's "attentional filter" of neurons assesses which data is most important and directs us where to focus our moment-by-moment attention. Daniel J. Levitin, *The Organized Mind: Thinking Straight in the Age of Information Overload* (New York: Dutton, 2014), 17.
2. Based on the work of psychotherapists Virginia Satir, Fritz Perls, and Milton Erickson and originally applied to the language we use, this Meta Model was developed by Richard Bandler and John Grinder in *The Structure of Magic,* vol. 1, *A Book About Language and Therapy* (Palo Alto, CA: Science and Behavior Books, 1975).

REFLECTION 2

1. Richard Rohr, *Falling Upward: A Spirituality for the Two Halves of Life* (San Francisco: Jossey-Bass, 2011), xxi.
2. Thomas Merton, *No Man Is an Island* (New York: Houghton Mifflin, 1955), xii.

3. Leonard Cohen, "Anthem," *The Future* (New York: Columbia, 1992), CD.

REFLECTION 3

1. Albert Ellis's Rational Emotive Behavior Therapy (REBT) and Aaron T. Beck's Cognitive Behavior Therapy (CBT), which evolved from REBT, are both based on aspects of Stoic philosophy.
2. Ryan Holiday's book *The Obstacle Is the Way: The Timeless Art of Turning Trials into Triumph* (New York: Portfolio/Penguin, 2014) explains the origins of Stoicism in Classical Antiquity and uses modern-day examples from business leaders like Steve Jobs. The book was very popular among professional athletes and coaches in the NFL. (Greg Bishop, "How a Book on Stoicism Became Wildly Popular at Every Level of the NFL," *Sports Illustrated,* December 7, 2015, www .si.com/nfl/2015/12/08/ryan-holiday-nfl-stoicism-book-pete-carroll -bill-belichick).
3. The title is adapted from *Meditations,* written by Roman emperor Marcus Aurelius.

REFLECTION 5

1. "What Is Contemplation?" *Center for Action and Contemplation,* https://cac.org/about-cac/what-is-contemplation/.

REFLECTION 8

1. Richard Rohr, *Immortal Diamond: The Search for Our True Self* (San Francisco: Jossey-Bass, 2013), 190.
2. Rohr, *Immortal Diamond,* 190.
3. Rohr, *Immortal Diamond,* 191.
4. Rohr, *Immortal Diamond,* 191.
5. Brené Brown, *The Gifts of Imperfection: Let Go of Who You Think You're Supposed to Be and Embrace Who You Are* (Center City, MN: Hazelden, 2010), ix.
6. Rohr, *Immortal Diamond,* 191.

REFLECTION 9

1. Richard Rohr, *Falling Upward: A Spirituality for the Two Halves of Life* (San Francisco: Jossey-Bass, 2011), xvii.

REFLECTION 14

1. Studies cited in Deb A. Dana, *The Polyvagal Theory in Therapy: Engaging the Rhythm of Regulation* (New York: Norton, 2018), 187.

REFLECTION 15

1. Coleman Barks, trans., *The Essential Rumi* (New York: HarperCollins, 1995), 36.

REFLECTION 16

1. "Staying within Your Comfort Zone While Reflecting on Personal Suffering" is adapted from "Staying within Your Comfort Zone" in Patrick Boland, *The Universal Christ: How a Forgotten Reality Can Change Everything We See, Hope For, and Believe: Companion Guide for Individuals* (Albuquerque, NM: CAC Publishing, 2020), 23-25.

REFLECTION 17

1. Rohr, *Falling Upward,* 127–28.
2. Carl G. Jung, *Collected Works of C. G. Jung, Volume 7: Two Essays in Analytical Psychology,* trans. R.F.C. Hull (London: Routledge & Kegan Paul, 1953), 197.
3. Rohr, *Falling Upward,* 128.
4. Rohr, *Falling Upward,* 133.
5. Rohr, *Falling Upward,* 133.
6. Rohr, *Falling Upward,* 133.

REFLECTION 18

1. Carl G. Jung, *Collected Works of C. G. Jung, Volume 7: Two Essays in Analytical Psychology,* trans. R.F.C. Hull (London: Routledge & Kegan Paul, 1953), 197.
2. Mike McHargue, *Finding God in the Waves: How I Lost My Faith and Found It Again through Science* (New York: Convergent, 2016), 205.

REFLECTION 19

1. *C. G. Jung Letters, vol. 1,* selected and edited by Gerhard Adler (London: Routledge, 1972), 19, n. 8.

REFLECTION 20

1. Isabel Briggs Myers with Peter B. Myers, *Gifts Differing: Understanding Personality Type* (Palo Alto, CA: Consulting Psychologists Press, 1980).

REFLECTION 23

1. Blaise Pascal, *Pensées* (Paris: Librairie de Firmin Didot Frères, Fils et Cie, 1858) 74.
2. Kahlil Gibran, *The Prophet* (London: Heinemann, 1926), 16, 19.

REFLECTION 24

1. René Descartes, "*La Recherche de la Vérité par La Lumiere Naturale*" ("*The Search for Truth by Natural Light*"), 1647, https://fr.wikisource.org/wiki/Page:Descartes_-_Œuvres,_éd._Adam_et_Tannery,_X.djvu/535.

REFLECTION 30

1. Richard Rohr, *Adam's Return: The Five Promises of Male Initiation* (Spring Valley, N.Y: Crossroads, 2004).

REFLECTION 31

1. *The Cloud of Unknowing and Other Works,* trans. A. C. Spearing (London: Penguin, 2001), chap. 40.
2. "National Culture," *Hofstede Insights*, https://hi.hofstede-insights.com/national-culture.
3. "National Culture."

REFLECTION 38

1. The text to this self-guided sit is adapted from Boland, *The Universal Christ: Companion Guide for Individuals,* 15–21.

REFLECTION 39

1. As quoted in "Crisis Contemplation," *Center for Action and Contemplation,* June 11, 2020, https://cac.org/crisis-contemplation-2020-06-11/.
2. Richard Rohr, "Ascending and Descending Religions," *The Mendicant* 8, no. 3 (Summer 2018): 1, https://cac.org/wp-content/uploads/2018/08/theMendicant_Vol8No3.pdf.

About the Type

This book was set in Bembo, a typeface based on an old-style Roman face that was used for Cardinal Pietro Bembo's tract *De Aetna* in 1495. Bembo was cut by Francesco Griffo (1450–1518) in the early sixteenth century for Italian Renaissance printer and publisher Aldus Manutius (1449–1515). The Lanston Monotype Company of Philadelphia brought the well-proportioned letterforms of Bembo to the United States in the 1930s.

CENTER FOR ACTION AND CONTEMPLATION

Amidst a time of planetary change and disruption, we envision a recovery of our deep connection to each other and our world, led by Christian and other spiritual movements that are freeing leaders and communities to overcome dehumanizing systems of oppression and cooperate in the transforming work of Love. —CAC Vision Statement

Founded in 1987, the Center for Action and Contemplation (CAC) is located in the South Valley of Albuquerque, New Mexico. The CAC has served an international constituency for over thirty years, supporting Franciscan Fr. Richard Rohr's world-renowned ecumenical ministry. Fr. Richard is Founder of the CAC and the Academic Dean of the Center's Living School; his teachings are the basis of the organization's vision and ongoing work. Together with Fr. Richard, Cynthia Bourgeault, James Finley, Barbara Holmes, and Brian McLaren form the core faculty members of the CAC and Living School.

Our Mission
Open the door for a critical mass of spiritual seekers to experience the transformative wisdom of the Christian contemplative tradition and nurture its emergence in service to the healing of our world.

Contemplative Programs and Resources
- **Daily Meditations:** Free daily or weekly email reflections by Fr. Richard and guest teachers.
- **Online Education:** Self-paced online courses, including audio, video, and discussion.
- **Living School:** Two-year program (launched in 2013) combines onsite and online learning.
- **Podcasts:** Discussion of inspirational topics with Richard Rohr, CAC faculty, staff, and guests.
- **CAC Bookstore:** A wide selection of faculty books, recordings, and CAC's journal, *Oneing*.

The question for us is always, "How can we turn information into transformation?" How can we use the sacred texts, tradition, and experience to lead people into new places with God, with life, and with themselves? —Richard Rohr

To learn more about the Center for Action and Contemplation, please visit https://cac.org/.

The Universal Christ: Related Products

The Universal Christ Companion Guide for Groups

The Companion Guide for Groups has been designed for those who wish to gather in a small group to engage in contemplative practices inspired by Richard Rohr's book *The Universal Christ*. Three group guides and a facilitator's guide are included in the 172-page book. To learn more about and to purchase *The Universal Christ Companion Guide for Groups*, published by CAC Publishing, visit store.cac.org.

The Universal Christ Companion Guide for Individuals

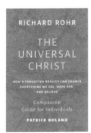

The Companion Guide for Individuals has been designed for those who wish to deepen their experience of the Universal Christ in daily life. This 226-page guide provides multiple points of engagement with each chapter of Richard Rohr's book *The Universal Christ*. To learn more about and to purchase *The Universal Christ Companion Guide for Individuals*, published by CAC Publishing, visit store.cac.org.

Every Thing Is Sacred:
40 Practices and Reflections on the Universal Christ

Every Thing Is Sacred is a series of reflections that invite the reader to further explore the content and themes of Richard Rohr's book *The Universal Christ*. Ideal as a Lenten devotional or an accompaniment on a retreat, this book of reflections includes practical exercises for the reader to examine their faith journey. To learn more about and to purchase *Every Thing Is Sacred*, published by SPCK, visit spck.org.uk.